WESTCOUNTRY WORDS & WAYS

K. C. Phillipps

DAVID & CHARLES
NEWTON ABBOT   LONDON   NORTH POMFRET (VT)   VANCOUVER

For My Mother and Father

ISBN 0 7153 7025 1

Library of Congress Catalog Card Number 76–4365

Set in 11 on 13pt Linotype Baskerville and printed in
Great Britain by Latimer Trend & Company Ltd Plymouth
for David & Charles (Publishers) Limited
Brunel House   Newton Abbot   Devon

Published in the United States of America
by David & Charles Inc
North Pomfret   Vermont 05053   USA

Published in Canada
by Douglas David & Charles Limited
1875 Welch Street   North Vancouver   BC

CONTENTS

3

ABBREVIATIONS

The following abbreviations are used in the text:

EDD *The English Dialect Dictionary*
ME Middle English (c1150–1470)
OE Old English (up to 1150)
OED *The Oxford English Dictionary*
SED *Survey of English Dialects*

NOTE: In the interests of readability and to avoid too fragmentary a text, more than one word has been included under a single heading, but the index should enable each word discussed to be located. With a similar aim of avoiding a disrupted text, notes and references have not been numbered but are listed separately with a series of catchwords.

INTRODUCTION

For over a hundred years now the English dialects have been on the wane. The diarist and minor Victorian poet A. J. Munby, whose memoirs entitled *Munby, Man of Two Worlds* appeared in 1972, was uncomfortably accurate in what he prophesied, as long ago as 1860, on the impending decline of dialect: 'It is the dark side, among many blessings, of our railway days; which will ultimately destroy all refreshing ruggedness, all the valuable folk-lore, of our rural dialects, and all the charming differentia – or what little that is left – of our rustic dress and manners. God forbid that one should live to such a time, when all England shall be one dead level of Americanised half-educated vulgarity.' The upshot of such concern, echoed also by the great Victorian dialectologist A. J. Ellis, whose volumes on *Early English Pronunciation* (1869–74) were appearing at this time, was the formation in 1873 of the English Dialect Society. In the next twenty-three years eighty glossaries were produced by the society, whose activities culminated in the *magnum opus* of England's greatest dialectician, Joseph Wright – *The English Dialect Dictionary,* published in six volumes.

The production of this work in Oxford by Wright and his team of assistants in the record time of ten years, from 1896 to 1905, has been a standing reproach to tardier lexicographers ever since. It has, of course, been much criticised, but on any account it is a magnificent achievement. I would commend it, especially, as the most compulsively readable dictionary I know. The tendency, we are told, of modern dialect study is to see words against their total background, but there is nothing new under the sun, for this was the supreme merit of Wright's dictionary, published seventy years ago. Reading it conjures up the vanished world of the British countryside, in all its virtues and defects, affording the reader that characteristic contradictory experience of the present – a nostalgic sigh for the loss of a rich cultural heritage, together with a feeling of relief that life is now easier. Those who peruse its pages have a choice between great store of proverbial wisdom and innumerable abusive epithets; between directions for many dubious and sometimes horrific remedies and rules for harmless indoor and outdoor games; they will also learn the countless ways in which their ancestors, in a hand-to-mouth economy, wasted nothing in their surroundings, washing blankets in urine, using dogs' droppings to remove hair from hides when tanning, making whistles out of sycamore twigs, *tatie-guns* out of a slice of potato and a goose-quill and pan-scourers from bundles of heather, or converting a pig's bladder into a musical instrument, a football or a container for lard – 'puffed up like a bladder o' lard', as we still say in the South West of a conceited person.

More recently the *Survey of English Dialects,* emanating from Leeds and conducted by a team of fieldworkers asking questions throughout England from a questionnaire prepared by Harold Orton and Eugen Dieth, is concerned with the same kind of language that Wright chiefly recorded; the sort of English that is spoken by elderly working-class people in rural communities. The survey had a different kind of viewpoint from the *EDD*; a conspectus of dialect in which lexical items were duly balanced by other factors, with a welcome focus upon idiom and syntax. The three volumes for the southern counties, from fieldwork undertaken mainly in the 1950s, appeared in 1967–8, and not a moment too soon. In the half-century between the *EDD* and the *SED,* two world wars, affluence and snobbery, education and travel, and perhaps above all 'the media', have been powerful eroding factors. There have been enormous losses, yet 'though much is taken, much abides', as the survey clearly shows – especially when it deviates from its rather constricting programme to include idioms and explanatory details not strictly within its brief. It is gratifying, for instance, that in West Cornwall the

6

answer to the question 'What do you call any running water smaller than a river?' is, 'A river; we do call 'em all rivers; they aren't but streams.' Miss M. A. Courtney had made the same point about West Cornwall 'rivers' in 1890.

It is a measure of the way in which the study of language has been set on an uncompromisingly scientific basis over the last two generations that the *SED* is almost entirely written in phonetic transcriptions, and rightly so. No other method, least of all our wayward English spelling, could convey closely enough the sounds uttered, and it is well worth acquiring the International Phonetic Alphabet in order to derive full benefit from the survey. Yet many general readers, including many interested dialect speakers, do not include learning the IPA among the 'uses of literacy'; and thus one of the main functions of the older (and often much more amateurish) glossaries, to justify the dialect speaker in the validity and prestige of his special language, goes by default. In this way, English rural speech is brought a little nearer to extinction, though the presence of specimens embalmed on recording tape in the BBC archives is some compensation. In writing this book, which is concerned with vocabulary and idiom more than with sounds, I have tried to avoid phonetics, with the general reader and especially the westcountry reader, rather than the dialectician, in mind.

Perhaps the most valuable, and also the most innovatory, part of the *SED* is the third volume, which is largely concerned with idiom and usage. Let us suppose, for instance (it was one of the survey questions), that we wished to say, in Devon or Cornwall, that something cost almost a pound. 'Near 'nough a pound' or 'purdy nigh a pound' might occur to us. 'Tight on a pound', from North Devon, is perhaps less predictable, as is 'shaking up', which the survey also records. If we doubt this, we have only to look at their Cornish quotations: 'He's shaking up seventy', or 'Nineteen shillings; that's shaking up a pound.' Most westcountrymen will probably agree that it does not take much spending nowadays to give a pound 'a brave shaking up', and it does not take many

7

replies like this to convince us that, within its scope, the SED is penetrating and authentic.

Not, of course, that the survey is the only source for idiom. The best writers in dialect, such as Charles Lee and Anne Treneer for Cornwall, or Eden Phillpotts and A. J. Coles ('Jan Stewer') for Devon, all 'watched points' very closely. Also one must not forget the broadcaster who has probably done more than anyone else in the last few years to keep alive the Cornish dialect – Mrs Hilda Rowse of Newlyn East. In a recent short story in *Cornish Nation*, the magazine of Mabyon Kernow, she describes a spinster who has got herself ready for an outing which may have matrimonial prospects as 'all tiched up with her ear-rings'. You will not find *tiched up with* in this sense in any glossary that I know of, but for mid-Cornwall, at least, how right it is!

If I do not include Sir Arthur Quiller-Couch among the most reliable of sources for dialect it is from no lack of fondness for one of the greatest of Cornish scholars and men of letters. Rather it is that Q is too inventive to record dialect faithfully. A character like Caleb Trotter in *The Astonishing History of Troy Town* speaks too lively a version of the vernacular for our purposes. He owes a good deal to Sam Weller, particularly Weller's trick of beginning with an everyday phrase and then suggesting an imaginary speaker and circumstance when the phrase might be heard: 'on'y a figger o' speech, sir, and nothin' to do wi' the yarn, as the strollin' actor said when this theayter catched a-fire'. As a matter of fact this pattern is native to the South West as well as to the Wellers – 'all so gay, as Bully said when he tarred the stove', or 'every little helps, as the woman said when she piddled in the sea' – but it would be unwise to take many of these, or any other figures and turns of phrase, as anything but the product of Q's lively inventiveness.

He is sometimes content with recording, for when he writes of St Neot in 'St Piran and the Visitation', 'He's as big as bull's beef, is St Neot, ever since he worked that miracle over the fishes', Q is faithfully recording a phrase of difficult interpretation, still frequently heard, 'so big as bull's beef', meaning

8

very conceited. Even here, however, the positioning of *is St Neot* is northern not westcountry usage and comes of Q's wide reading. Again, when Q describes a boisterous man in another story from the same volume as 'a great red rory-cum-tory chap', he may be recording a dialect meaning of 'boisterous' (though the more usual meaning of *rory-tory* in the South West is 'gaudy', or 'garishly flamboyant'), but the form with the additional *cum* is, I suspect, a piece of embroidery on Q's part. Nevertheless, this probably bogus word occurs in the *OED*, though Wright was too shrewd to quote Q in this instance in the *EDD*. On the other hand, Wright does quote Caleb Trotter's verb to *paradise* for to *parody*, which has no more validity in a dictionary than Mrs Malaprop's *'allegory* on the banks of the Nile'.

In her biography of her husband Joseph, Elizabeth Wright describes the old man listening for a while to various broadcasts about, or making use of, dialect, and then calling out irritably, 'Switch him off; he knows nowt about it!' One understands this irritation; for example, in a recent play about the 1913 china-clay strike it was annoying to hear BBC playwrights labouring under the delusion that in the West *likely* is used in the sense of 'probably' in a sentence such as 'He'll likely not be home till late' (usage from Yorkshire down to Leicestershire, according to the *EDD*). What is heard, in fact, is 'He won't be home till late, more'n likely', and in 1913 the dialect speaker would add, as my grandparents did, an extra 'd' to the last word – *more'n likely'd* – perhaps by association with 'likelihood'. The BBC 2 production of Zola's *Germinal*, set in a putative Black Country, was carefully checked for dialect, but, typically, no one researches the dialect of the far South West.

There is little doubt that the folk-life of a nation is in one respect the opposite of life in the human body; the extremities tend to die last. The area which I call the westcountry, meaning specifically, as the *Oxford English Dictionary* allows, the far south-western peninsula (more especially the area west of Exeter), has until recently been remote enough and rugged enough to preserve its own individuality. Despite much variety

9

of custom and vociferous local rivalries, the accidents of history and geography determine that the whole area west of Exeter has a basic homogeneity along its 100 miles of length: a sea-girt promontory whose granite spine and dramatic northern coastline contrast with the lush river valleys reaching to the south coast. Throughout the area, though in different proportions as we go *upward* (east) into England, we find scattered hamlets and farmsteads of Celtic settlement, with their small, irregular fields, overlaid by larger, more nucleated villages on a later Anglo-Saxon pattern. The westcountry is not yet part of the Home Counties, and for a few years more an unimproved Exeter bypass may spare us the worst ignominies of being commuter territory for an ever-greater London.

Not, apparently, that we wish to be spared anything, as we rush to embrace nonentity without realising that in the kind of special ancestral vocabulary that is the subject of this book we have a series of keepsakes far more valuable than most of the 'souvenirs' at our seaside emporia. 'You'm out of date,' a mid-Cornwall acquaintance proudly told me when I started writing articles on the dialect of Cornwall in *The Western Morning News*, 'we don't belong to use they old words down here now!' It is not surprising, then, that as we turn the pages of Joseph Wright's Dictionary we find many westcountry sentences that are baffling. It would be interesting to test Devonian or Cornish speakers under the age of forty on specimen sentences like these:

'I got a most bedoling pain in my teeth and chacks all round to my nuddick.'
''Twas so clisty that the gruter would hardly turn the coam.'
'You can't use barley-doust vur bed-tyes, cuz tha iles would run into 'ee.'

It is not difficult to see why so much of this language is becoming meaningless. Driven by the power of a modern tractor, the *gruter* will turn the *coam* however *clisty* the soil may be; the foam mattress has superseded both the doust bed-tye and the feather tye, and the most *bedoling* bodily pain may yield to better medical treatment. Improved living conditions are implicit in these linguistic losses, and no sensible person would wish things to be otherwise; but surely all the older language need not now be thought too unsophisticated to use. One of the sadder effects of advancing technology has been the cutting off of direct links of experience with the past, and a consequent severance from the literature of the past which reflected this life. The story of Ruth the gleaner, for example (*leasing* was a common dialect equivalent to 'gleaning'), probably ceased to correspond to most westcountrymen's experience from about the beginning of this century. With changing techniques, generations are arising among farming communities who, as one farmer put it, 'don't know a stiddle from a staddle'.

Dialect is not always a lively vehicle of communication, though at its best it is. 'They had hundreds of proverbs and sayings, and their talk was stiff with simile', wrote Flora Thompson of the men she knew in the hamlet of 'Lark Rise'. While this is true, there has also always been a repetitive element in dialect utterance, which can be almost liturgically restful or maddeningly monotonous, depending on one's mood. It is a difficult art to convey the humorous effects of tedium without being tedious, but Charles Lee, who has recorded our dialect more amusingly than any other writer despite his non-Cornish origin, manages it successfully in *Our Little Town*:

> 'Fine night,' says the stranger casually. Jan fixes him with a pair of blinking blue eyes, and makes answer—'Ess. Moon's looking beautiful tonight – beautiful and bright she's looking. 'Tis light enough of a night when there's a moon. When there an't no moon, then 'tis dark. But when there's a moon, then 'tis tolerable bright, you see.'
> The stranger assents, and innocently conceiving the subject to be exhausted, remarks that the night is also somewhat chilly. But Jan . . . continues blandly – 'Ess. Very different when there edn' no moon; then 'tis dark, sure enough. When there's a nice bright moon, then you can see your way about, b'lieve. But these dark nights, they'm terrible dark, I assure 'ee. Sometimes you couldn' see nothing, these dark nights when there edn' no moon.'

The speaker in this passage is a man and, as any dialectician will tell you, it is men rather than women who make the best and most spontaneous dialect informants. To quote Harold Orton, editor of the *SED*: 'In this country men speak the vernacular more frequently, more consistently and more genuinely than women.' Lee, for example, will have learnt many of his keenly observed phrases and figures of speech in the Falcon Inn at Mawgan-in-Pydar, the village where he lived for a year. Nevertheless, in the South West the influence of the village pub can, or at least could, be exaggerated. Such exaggeration overlooks the influence – formerly very powerful – of the chapels, and of societies like the Western Temperance League, emanating from Bristol. The idea of the pub as the centre of village life is something of a northern and south-eastern stereotype. Sir John Betjeman, who always sees through the stereotype to reality, notes this about Port Isaac: 'The Community Centre is all wrong by Town Planning standards. It is not the public-house, but the Liberal Club. Anyone who knows Cornish fishermen must know that most of them do not drink, many are chapel-goers and a Liberal Club without a licence is the sort of place where you would expect to find them.' Some such club, more often than not known as the Institute, was, and still is, to be found in many south-western villages, and in my experience it is here that dialect can be heard in full flower.

The Institute generally had two rooms – a reading-room, for any individuals who were maladjusted enough to aspire to greater literacy (thereby earning for themselves ironic nicknames like 'Doctor' and 'Lawyer'), and a billiard-room. The latter was always the popular room, though not patronised by everyone – not by heroes in the books of those former best-selling novelists Joseph and Silas Hocking, for example:

The smoke-room and billiard-room he generally shunned. Not that he objected to smoking or billiard-playing, but because they were so crowded and hot and reeking, while the reading-room was cool and quiet, and generally speaking unoccupied; and so, while his companions were showing their proficiency in the use of the cue, he was storing his mind with facts and philosophies.

12

In the billiard-room, a less lofty tone prevailed. The way to secure attention there in any narrative was by frequent use of the appellative 'O' man' (like Mr Polly's friend Parsons in H. G. Wells's novel) and a liberal sprinkling of blood: 'Cor da hell, o' man, when I catched up that bloody gun, o' man, and fired across that bloody field, o' man, you couldn't see that rabbit's arse for dust!' To offset the monotony, however, one might collect some memorable gaffe or Cornubian–Irish bull, lovingly reported, or even new-minted, as perpetrated by the kind of speakers who 'don't know 'nough to know they don't know nothing'. One might hear such pronouncements as this judgement on a good hit at cricket: 'If that hedge wudn' there he'd a gone right through 'un'; or the fond mother's concern for her son: 'John, 'tis cold, come in and put on your hat; if you never had a hat you'd be wearin' of 'n all the time.' A clay-captain who was prone to such 'forth and back' utterance is quoted as having announced, in threatening tones: 'There's a man 'ere today idn' come; if he don't come tomorrow, I shall send 'un home!' 'See they two houses,' a village idiot explained to visitors, 'well, I live in the middle one!' Best of all perhaps, is a gloomy prophecy still remembered as having been made on the occasion of an early aviator being lost over the Sahara desert: 'Bloody sharks have got 'e by this times!'

In his volume of essays *From a Cornish Window* Q quotes his old schoolmaster at Clifton, the Manx poet T. E. Brown, to support his opinion that only Scots dialects have the authority upon which successful literature can be based: 'The Ayrshire dialect has a *Schwung* and a confidence that no English county can pretend to. Our dialects are apologetic things, half-ashamed, half-insolent. Burns has no doubts.' One would wish to enter a caveat for William Barnes of Dorset but on the whole Brown, who himself wrote poetry in the Manx dialect, was right. The phrase 'half-ashamed, half-insolent' is also a piece of sound diagnosis, and by and large, the insolence and impropriety have never been recorded – not for Cornwall, at least, until 1971 when, writing in *The Cornish Review*, Ithell Colquhoun listed sentences like: 'The Devil shits luck

13

for some, but when he come to we, he's hard-bound.' She also reports, of the phrase 'fitting exactly, like Tom Rowe's mouth', that an old woman expostulated with the village postmaster for 'telling such things to the lady'. 'I am not sure,' Miss Colquhoun comments, 'whether she was afraid my attitude might be derisive or condescending, or whether the phrase had a double entendre which scandalised her.'

Most of the dialect glossaries were made in the nineteenth century when the idiosyncrasies of dialect still flourished, but when the barometer of public opinion was set against coarseness of all kinds; and moreover, the dialecticians of those days were often ladies. We can sometimes guess from the replies that their informants are not telling all:

> 'It was so dark,' she said, 'that had she gone "Jan Dark" would have carried her off.' I asked who 'Jan Dark' was. 'Oh, no-one, Miss Courtney; it is only a saying in the country.'

Mrs Sarah Hewett, recording for Devonshire, will tell you more than Miss Margaret Courtney, for West Cornwall; even so, the class barrier is still there: 'No, mum, us niver useth the buzzymilk. Tidden gude vur nort.' No phrase epitomised the barrier more than one which is almost never heard nowadays – 'making so bold':

> 'Who was she then, makin' so bold?'
> 'I don't know her name.'

For better or for worse, we no longer apologise for 'boldness'. In a franker and more democratic age, the *SED* fieldworkers felt able to ask questions like 'What do you call this that you sit on?' One can imagine the giggling, the embarrassment, the pretence at being scandalised; yet these words have always played a bigger part in dialect than in standard English, and some of them, with many lively idioms, will die with it.

There has always been, in the South West, a preponderance of scatological over sexual frankness. It seems that the 1972 Northcott Theatre production of an English version of part of the Cornish *Ordinalia* scandalised some of its westcountry audiences, but the outspoken phrases on excretory subjects

14

that may have given offence were all in the text, figuring there as prominently as they do in the modern dialect. When Norris, translating the plays for his edition of 1859, has one of the executioners say:

> Thou strikest like a dirty fellow
> Thou art better fitted
> *To do any other dirty work . . .*

he is bowdlerising:

> ty a wor guel *bremmyn bras*
> *dyllo menough mes a'th tyn*

that is, 'frequently to let a great fart from thine arse'. This, doubtless, is the language a fourteenth-century audience would have taken in their stride.

Refinement is not necessarily virtue, nor is coarseness of expression necessarily vice. Wright quotes in the *EDD* a sentence from Exmoor: 'Put it up 'pon the *arse* of the wagon', where the word merely means the back part. I once heard a local preacher of great virtue and sagacity remark of a fine day that ended in rain, 'Well, the day have pissed her own heels, sur 'nough'; while a stout old Cornishman, who had rung the bells in the parish church for over fifty years and who was so staunch a churchman as to have earned the nickname of 'Canon', once made use of this comparison as I clumsily tied up a parcel with rope: 'Boy, that's strong, but 'tis not very neat; like a bull's arse sewed up with a chain!'

Few dialects are as rich as those of the South West in simile. For a parallel inventiveness in appropriate, or ironically inappropriate, comparisons, we must turn to the Hebrew tradition as recorded in the Bible. When, for instance, we compare 'You don't want it no more'n a toad want side-pockets', or 'You'm awkward, like a cow handling a musket' with biblical phrases about camels going through the eyes of needles, we discern a strong affinity in both the humour and the uninhibited exaggeration.

A sharp observation of both nature in general and human nature in particular forms the basis of many of these comparisons. When anyone looking cold and woebegone is compared to a *winnard,* ie a redwing, the ornithology is as keen as Gilbert White's, who noted in 1771: 'Redwings are some of the first birds that suffer with us in severe weather.' (A bleak *four-turnings* on the St Breock Downs, where the St Austell–Padstow and St Columb–Wadebridge roads meet, is known as Winnard's Perch.) Of a man with an unfortunate resemblance to an ape in both appearance and behaviour, an uncharitable but perceptive neighbour is said to have remarked, 'When thicky fellow start to clap for his-self, we shall know that he really *is* a monkey.' Dialect speakers draw on a common 'bank' of peasant observation going back hundreds of years. We may think that the way of describing a disjointed utterance – 'in jerks, like a pig pissing' – is not worth noting, but yet it is of interest that the expression had already been recorded in the seventeenth century by gossip and antiquarian John Aubrey: 'Now Dr. Kettle was wont to say that Seneca writes as a boare does pisse; *scilicet* by jirkes.' A dialect simile may even represent that last vestige of a long and noble tradition. Mocking comparisons, never more appropriate than today, of a person with an untidy head of hair to 'an owl looking out of an ivy-bush' recall to the student of earlier English that favourite *mise-en-scène* of medieval literature:

> Tho stod an old stok thar byside
> Thar the owle song hire tyde,
> And wes mid ivi al bigrowe
> Hit wes thare owle erdingstowe.

Personal idiosyncrasies are also closely observed. When I went as an undergraduate to Liverpool, I was told by a villager who had stayed there during the last war: 'Liverpool's a rough city; you'll find that even the charladies do carry their brooms at the ready under their arm, like a little sporting gun.' I was warned later, when I showed an interest in what are often called folk-life studies: 'You don't want to become like one of these here fellas with a beard and a curly pipe.' In his book *Twenty Years at St Hilary* Father Bernard Walke describes the St Hilary congregation's reaction when an even more convinced Anglo-Catholic than himself visited his pulpit: 'There's old Wason over to Cury. He's a proper old Roman Catholic they do say . . . Can 'ee see'n my dear? The one wearing a hat like a tea-cosy.' Walke's comment is: 'Why a biretta should be described as a tea-cosy, I do not know.' (Not a bad comparison at all, I should have thought.) Many of these similes, as we have already seen, are neither charitable nor for the drawing-room; if one's victim's mouth is too big, it is 'like a jail door'; if pursed and screwed up, it is 'like a duck's fert' (*fert* being a common, but hitherto unrecorded, word for the anus).

We can see, by reading Anne Treneer's autobiographical books, how a lively, high-spirited family evolved their own bywords, which could sometimes take on a wider currency:

Old Mrs Beard was once embarrassed by an 'article' which she had bought and which refused to conceal its form in the wrappings . . . a nice little article with roses round. Contrary to promise, Mr Beard never came to meet and support her. She kept on saying 'Where's feyther to? I can't think why feyther id'n 'ere', a saying we kept up in the family for years. Whenever any arrangement went awry, we would say, 'Where's feyther to?'

A convenient phrase to excuse burnt food which survived for years in one family I know was 'that's how Caleb like it', from a long-distant time when an apologetic chapel member brought burnt buns to a 'faith tea' with the explanation, 'That's how Caleb like 'em!'

From situations like this, in a community where life was lived more publicly than today, innumerable phrases arise. The journal *Old Cornwall* is full of them; some very localised, others more widespread. Often they refer to events long past; for example, 'I'm in my own light, like the Mayor of Market-Jew' relates to an earlier building than the present parish church of Market-Jew (Marazion) in which the Mayor sat on a very high seat with his back to the window. The phrase 'like Blacker, who had occasion for the whole', refers to an elector in the days of bribery who was shown a pile of money and told to take what he had occasion for; his reply has become proverbial to describe anyone who is too grasping. A worrier in the china-clay area is 'always going Castle to meet trouble coming from St Columb', Castle being the mid-Cornwall Castle-an-Dinas, a huge earthwork which is still impressive, even in competition with nearby china-clay dumps. An event that is soon over is said to be 'like Lostwithiel market; begin half-past twelve, finish one o'clock'. The wife of an alleged Mathy Moyle, on looking at an old horse that her husband had bought at a fair, was provoked to a comment that has made her name a byword on the subject of niggardly deals: 'Thee's might's well gov'd half-crown more, and bought a good one while thee'st 'bout it.'

As the racial memory becomes blurred by excess of new and more cosmopolitan impressions, there is a tendency to confer anonymity on the proverbial figures of dialect speech – 'like th'old fella said'. Who were they originally, these worthies – Lady Fan Todd, dressed to death and killed with fashion; Sal Hatch, similarly attired; Straight Jane from Cork (or from the workhouse); Stone Dunk from Dublin (of any unfamiliar or outlandish figure); Dicky, Dicky Dout with his shirt hanging out; the passon's fool, who liked anything that was good? Tyrannised as we now are by facts and timetables, we are fast losing – if we have not already lost – the habit of instant metaphor. In an age increasingly wedded to the exactness of science and technology, the limitation which Blake foretold is very much with us:

May God us keep
From single vision and Newton's sleep.

Metaphor came much more naturally to the dialect speaker. In the West, for example, one expressed sympathy with an insoluble personal problem with some such phrase as 'everybody do knaw what to do with a kicking horse except he that got'n'. If grief over bereavement seemed excessive, people recalled the proverb: 'A roaring cow do soon forget her calf', and if someone mended a tear hastily, it was said to be 'run up with a red-hot needle and burning thread'. Those who

18

raked up old scandals were reminded that 'the more you meddle with an old turd, the worse he stink'; while those who both grumbled and were irresponsible were told: 'The worst spoke in the wheel crake (squeaks) first.' The south-western equivalent of 'softly, softly catchee monkey' is 'you don't beat a drum to catch a mouse'; and a proverb like 'never have a wishbone where your backbone ought to be' is almost a sermon in itself. I remember one old farmer's wife telling another in the lean inter-war years, 'With eggs, you don't see a new penny for an old one', and in those days new pennies and old pennies had the same value.

Sadly, the modern writer who aspires to dialect has less and less experienced speech to draw on. In these latter days of the vernacular there has been one last, fine flourish of dialect writing in Anne Treneer's two tales 'Happy Button' and 'Old Mr Trebilcock', and Mrs Hilda Rowse and the frequent prize-winner of the Gorsedd, the octogenarian Mr W. J. Hawken, continue to produce faithful and interesting writing. For the rest, we can only echo the biblical motto of the Federation of Old Cornwall Societies: 'Gather up the fragments that remain, that nothing be lost!'

ABROAD

This word is more common in the dialects of the South West than in standard English. It is a sign of widening horizons that for the last two centuries *abroad* has increasingly tended to mean, in English, 'out of the country', whereas in Henry Carey's song 'Sally in Our Alley' the swain declares his intention 'to walk abroad with Sally', meaning merely 'out of the house'. In the South West the word means (of the mouth) 'wide open' and (of one's coat) 'unbuttoned'; 'He sat there, mouth abroad, catching flies'; 'his coat is all abroad'. We can compare these instances with biblical usage, such as 'Moses spread abroad his hands' (Exodus 10: 33).

The *EDD* records idiomatic uses of *gone abroad,* in the sense of 'gone to pieces, or dissolved', in sentences like 'I wish they'd make haste; the potatoes is all gone abroad, and the pilchards is spoiling', and (from the context of jam-making, obviously) 'the sugar has gone abroad'.

AFTERGRASS

There can be few phrases that are quite as unauthentic as the bookish expression 'hay-making'. *Saving* hay is more appropriate to the uncertainties of the Cornish climate, and there is something in this frequently heard phrase of the self-congratulatory parsimony in the Cornish character; the parsimony of those accustomed for generations to wresting a living from a not always kindly land. In the West, before the advent of the hay-baler, farmers were often occupied for weeks "bout the hay', and they generally had specialised expressions for all the individual operations: *cutting* hay, for instance; *turning* hay with pikes or hay-forks; *kicking* hay with a mechanical hay-kicker; *pooking* hay, ie putting it, when sufficiently dry, into small piles or *pooks,* in case of rain; *herding of it in*, ie putting it in long piles 3ft high, known as *drams* (perhaps the most interesting word, to the comparative philologist, in the Cornish dialect). These *drams* often covered the whole length of the field, and were convenient for pitching, as the wagon went between; though in a *catchy* season it might be necessary to *pook* up again from the *drams*. At length they came to the stage of *carring* (carrying) the hay; raking the *arrish* (stubble) and hoping for rain to bring on the *aftergrass,* or *aftermath* as the books say, though I have never heard the word used in the South West, nor have I heard *haycocks* for what we call *pooks*.

If the hay was too wet the rick might *het,* or be set alight by spontaneous combustion. *Het* is still heard as a variant for both 'heat' and 'heated': mist on a fine summer morning is sometimes said to be 'all for het and pichards'; despite the proverb, the blacksmith prides himself on dealing with as many irons in the fire as possible – 'in the one het' – and there is an expression *het broth,* used for anything (especially any entertainment) that is stale or has been seen before.

One custom of the hayfield that many will remember is vividly described by Sabine Baring-Gould in his novel *Red Spider*: 'The field rang with laughter, and occasional screams, as a man twisted a cord of hay, cast the loop round a girl's neck, drew her head towards him and kissed her face. That is called "the making of sweet hay".' In mid-Cornwall it is called 'making the hay sweet', but it amounts to the same thing, no doubt.

AGAIN(ST)

These two words, in the abbreviation *gin* or *ginst,* are very terse but meaningful conjunctions; one-word substitutes for 'by the time that': 'Gin you swep' up and turned round, 'tis dinner-time'; 'Ginst we got there, 'twas getting dark'. As a preposition, *again* can also mean 'near' or 'beside' or 'by the time of': 'His house is in the church-town, right *agin* the church'; 'They dashels 'll quailee gin tomorrow' (those thistles will wither by tomorrow). In his account of St Austell Canon Hammond relates that a deaf old woman told the vicar that she heard better in church 'since I 'ave a set agin the fowl' (ie the lectern).

ANGLEDITCH

According to Carew's *Survey* there is a fish peculiar to Devon and Cornwall, called a *shoat*: 'In shape and colour he resembleth the trout, howbeit in bigness and goodness cometh far behind him; his baits are flies and tag-worms, which the Cornish English term *angle-twitches*.' In Middle English we find the Cornishman Trevisa writing: 'Molles hunt *Angyltwytches* vnder erthe', and we can trace this word for a worm back still further to the Anglo-Saxon *angeltwicce. Angleditch* is the modern dialect form, used notably in the comparison: 'Sit still; you'm wriggling like a angleditch.'

Many other creatures figure in Cornish comparisons: a stupid person is 'as silly as a waggon 'oss'; a tactless one is 'as fore-right as a 'oss'. We can run out of the door quickly 'like a long dog' (ie one of the greyhound or whippet variety); we can be rumped up 'like a hedgehog', or be sick 'as a shag'; we can stare 'like a stat' (stoat) or 'like a sticked pig' (ie one that has been *sticked* or 'killed'); we can be dominated by our wives 'like a toad under a harrow'. We may be said to screech 'like a whitneck' – white-throated weasel – all weasels being noted for screaming, spitting or hissing when threatened or attacked. Another defence mechanism of this family of animals (stoat, weasel and polecat) is to release a powerful unpleasant scent from the glands under the tail; hence the simile 'stinking like a fitcher' (ie a fitchew or polecat). If we walk in an ungainly fashion, or present a bedraggled or dishevelled appearance, we are 'like a crab going to jail' (I have also heard 'like a crab going to Ireland'). If we are half-witted through being flustered, we might be described as 'like a hen afore day', and if we are drenched with rain, we can be said to be 'as wet as a dishwasher' (ie a water-wagtail).

Those other-worldly creatures, the *piskies*, also appear in comparisons; people are still said to 'laugh like a pisky', to be *pisky-led* or *pisky-lated* if they get lost, and a fluttering clothes-moth is sometimes called a *pisky*. Presumably, too, it is a cross-eyed *pisky* who is alluded to when we say that anything crooked or awry is 'as squint as Lobb's eyes'.

BACKALONG

> Tom Pearse, Tom Pearse, lend me your grey mare,
> All along, down along, out along lea.
> For I want for to go to Widecombe Fair . . .

From a modern point of view, there seems to be too much fuss about direction in the second line of this song, but this is characteristic of earlier rural usage. A largely rural language, such as Welsh, is far more precise than modern English in the various particles that indicate direction. Today we have short-circuited our adverbs and prepositions: 'Come *over into* Macedonia and help us' said the vision to Paul (Acts 16: 9); 'Come *across to* Macedonia' is the New English Bible version. Down to at least the time of Shakespeare, it was not usual to say 'come here', and 'leave here' as well as 'stay here'; men distinguished with *hither* and *hence*.

In dialect much of this finer sense of direction has been preserved in prepositions, demonstratives and adverbs. In mid-Cornwall, for instance, there is a whole range of words, varying from locality to locality according to landscape and other factors, which only a native can use accurately. The only place I know well enough to be able to quote as an example is the village of Roche in the centre of Cornwall. ('Remote?' said one of Roche's leading citizens, interviewed in a recent West of England broadcast, 'How can it be remote in the very middle of Cornwall?') Roche is 600ft above sea level, and people living in Withiel or St Wenn (upland villages, but not so high) accordingly go 'up Roche'. Roche people, however, can go still higher to Hensbarrow at 1,000ft, and anyone living nearer Hensbarrow, at Trezaise for example, would talk of going 'down Roche'. Men have always talked of going 'down to the sea', and Roche people go 'down Newquay' and 'down beach' but not 'down Padstow', for though it is on the coast and no further than Newquay, it is less accessible, and so they go 'out Padstow'. A problem arises when the Roche villager needs to travel to St Dennis and Whitemoor, two other villages near or just above the tree-line. He solves

24

this problem with *over*: 'over St Dennis'. He goes *in* to a market town – 'in St Austell' or 'in St Columb' – though paradoxically, older speakers used *to* or *into* where there was no sense of direction and where we should now have *in* or *at*: 'He lives into Bodmin'.

The mid-Cornwall man goes *up*, perhaps socially as well as geographically, when he goes 'up Plymouth', 'up Exeter' or 'up London'. He can even use the adverb *upward* generally, meaning 'in England': 'upward, where times is brisk', as the saying goes. A final subtlety of direction is the use of the word *back*, implying direction to a fairly remote place arrived at in rather a roundabout way: for example, from Roche we go 'back Lockengate', reached from my place of birth by going 'down Bugle' and then 'back left'.

Such patterns can be repeated throughout Devon and Cornwall; any dialect speaker has only to think of his own usage to realise this. The magazine *Old Cornwall* reports a woman describing her native village of St Day as 'handy all round; I do go in town (Redruth), out Camborne, down Penzance, over Truro and up St Austell whenever I've a mind to'; while Dr Martin Harris, of the University of Salford, has noted the same awareness of orientation in the Dartmoor parish of South Zeal, where people speak of going 'up Exeter', 'down Tavistock', 'in Okehampton' and so on.

In the line from Widecombe Fair with which we began – 'all along, down along, out along lea' – we have the use of the suffix *-along* to give a sense of direction to adverbs. Once common in the South West, this usage is now dying out. Claude Berry entitled three chapters of his book on Cornwall 'Upalong and downalong', 'Backalong' and 'Homealong', the first and the last of these three being topographical in import and the middle one giving an historical perspective. *Backalong* (compare 'back in they days') usually refers to past time. There are other formations. Writing in *Old Cornwall*, J. Kelynach recalled: 'Newlyn town, like all other Cornish towns and villages, had its uplong and downlong, inlong and outlong. Inlong was at the north end, called the Nor'ard . . . Outlong was known as The Green, the south extremity of Newlyn.'

There is also a precise use of prepositions to describe the movement of the wind. If the wind is *out,* it means that it has veered to the north; if it has gone *back* (presumably *widdershins* or 'anticlockwise') it has reverted to the south west, one of the most prevailing directions, often bringing rain from the Atlantic. "Tis no good for 'ee to pray for fine weather with the wind back there,' a member of his congregation told a new minister.

'BAISSLY'

Certain words, like *teasy* and *beastly* (both of which have roughly the diphthong of standard English *name),* are much commoner in the South West than in standard English. *Beastly* is predicated of any kind of dirt or lack of hygiene, but is more often (unlike standard English) literal than metaphorical in application. Here is the redoubtable Sarah Hewett reporting Devon usage at the end of the last century (her examples are so good that I more than suspect her of having made them up!):

> Mary, du'ee take they billises away from thickee cheel. Her'th a-put the naws ob'm in 'er mouth and made 'erzel za baissly as a peg!

'People,' said one old Cornishman, 'is getting more beastly all the time. Backalong, they used to do their business at the bottom of the garden; then they moved the lavatory nearer the house, and now 'tis indoors, if you please, right up next to the bedroom!' The dialect phrase for diarrhoea, 'back-door trot', preserves the memory of more primitive sanitary arrangements.

But if *beastly* is more common in the South West than elsewhere, the northern and North Midlands use of *beast* for store cattle, as distinct from horses and sheep, is still not normal in Devon and Cornwall. A glance at any local cattle-market advertisement from these counties will reveal the general south-western word for horned cattle of either sex, viz *bullocks.*

There is plenty of evidence from the rhymes of earlier English poetry to show that the westcountry pronunciation of these *ea* words (or something like it) was formerly more wide-spread in the language. Cowper's hymn 'God moves in a mysterious way' rhymes *way* with *sea* ('He plants his footsteps in the sea'), and at the beginning of the eighteenth century, Pope rhymes *obey* and *tea,* in the well-known satirical couplet about Queen Anne:

> Here thou, great Anna, whom three realms obey
> Dost sometimes counsel take – and sometimes tea.

One still hears talk, in the Duchy, of 'a good cup *tay*' with the pronunciation which Pope's rhyme indicates.

Certain crude rhymes which used to be chanted by children in my native village still preserved the earlier pronunciation. To the rallying cry of 'Down Roche among the goats' the reply was 'Up Trezaise amongst the fleas'. Another amusing, if mildly improper, rhyme which bears out this old pronunciation was the reply to the accusation of having broken wind: 'First speaker, wind breaker'. In standard English, of course, most of these *ea* words are now pronounced as if they were *ee* words, though there are exceptions like *great, break, steak* and the archaic *yea.*

'BEAL'

In the South West there is a tendency for words ending in *-ill* to be pronounced as *-eal.* Thus *till* is often *teal* and *bill,* in the sense of a bird's beak, *beal,* notably in an unsentimental observation of nature which compares the flowers of the iris to *ducks' beals*: 'The trouble with old ducks' beals is they'm soon over.' This must be the Dorset pronunciation of the word as well, for on a map which Thomas Hardy drew of his Wessex, he names Portland Bill (so called because the projection of cliff resembles a bird's bill) as 'The Beal'.

But in dialect speech *beal* is also used as a verb, different in meaning from the standard English sense of 'to bill and coo'. If an egg is taken from the hen or foster-mother just before hatching, the tapping of the bird's beak inside can

27

be heard, and when a small hole appears in the shell, the egg is said to be *bealed*.

BEE NOR BAW

Every student of dialect has to be, like Shakespeare's Autolycus, 'a snapper-up of unconsidered trifles', for it is surprising how often a small phrase, casually thrown out, may shed light on past customs, or prove to have a better ancestry than one had imagined. 'Weak as water' is a common phrase, 'weaker'n tatie-water' – presumably the water in which potatoes have been boiled – a less common, more provincial one. But *tatie-water* was no conjectural fluid, as Richard Jefferies, who was so familiar with rural poverty in Wiltshire in the last century, knew: 'Pot liquor is a favourite soup. I have known cottagers actually apply at farmers' kitchens not only for pot liquor in which meat has been soddened, but for the water in which potatoes have been boiled – potato liquor – and sup it up with avidity. And this not at times of dearth and scarcity, but rather with relish.' Or again, a turn of phrase like 'She never said bee nor baw to it', meaning 'She remained arrogantly silent', is the kind of provincialism that is neglected today. Yet in Tudor times, if we are to believe the playwright Thomas Dekker, this was a metropolitan enough phrase to be found on the lips of the wife of a prospective (albeit parvenu) Lord Mayor of London:

Away she flung, never returned, nor saide bih nor bah.

BELONG

One of the most persistent idiosyncrasies of the Cornish dialect is the use of *belong* as an extra or auxiliary verb to indicate customary action. The *EDD* has examples like, 'I don't belong to sing that, it is not one of my songs'; 'I belong working to Wheal Jane'; 'I don't belong going to Church, but I will this once'.

The following anecdote, related in 1948, nicely illustrates the difference between dialect and standard on this point. 'Forty years ago the new Methodist minister at Perranporth borrowed a horse and trap with a boy to drive from a local farmer named Prout, and set off for a distant preaching appointment. When the spirited animal shied at some roadside object the minister was alarmed, but the boy made light of it, saying, "That's nawthun', he belong to shy." "Indeed," said the minister ruefully, "I thought it belonged to Mr Prout!"'

BOWED

The *bow* of a ship is the fore-end where the planks bend inwards to the prow, and in order for a person to *bow*, he must bend the body. On the whole modern usage of *bow* meaning 'to bend' is restricted in standard English to ceremonial contexts. In the South West, however, *bow* may be used of things also: 'Who bowed thicky handle?' is a Devon quotation from the *EDD*, and Cornwall has expressions like 'This poker is bowed at the end.' Earlier, such usage was standard, and is preserved in the old nursery rhyme 'London Bridge is Broken Down'. When it is suggested that the broken bridge be built up with iron and steel, the objection is raised that 'Iron and steel will bend and bow'.

It is this extra dialectal meaning of *bow* that makes possible the pun reported by Canon Hammond at the expense of the Callington of his day: 'Callington is said to be politest town in England, because the houses on one side of the street are for ever bowing to those on the other side.'

BRIEF

There are certain dialect expressions which would seem to be West of England in the widest sense, such as the saying 'She looked at me like a cow upon a bastard calf', which expresses mingled contempt and suspicion. This the *EDD* quotes from Shropshire, but I have often heard it in Cornwall. Also in the *EDD* Wright quotes a Dorset informant: 'Were I asked by a neighbour "Can you spare a few plants?" I should not ask what plants, but answer at once as to cabbages.' In Cornwall and Devon, at least, the questioner might omit the plural sign and ask 'Can you spare a few plant?' In the South West the unchanged plural is as natural as with *sheep* or *fish,* and I have seen a notice 'Plant for Sale' in a cottage window as far north as Ludlow in Shropshire. This is reminiscent of the collective use of *plant* in the industrial sense.

A still more widespread dialect expression found, and doubt-less necessary, in most rural areas in less affluent times, is the word *brief* in the special sense of 'a begging letter or petition'. A Shropshire quotation given in the *OED* will serve as a definition for the South West also: 'A writing setting forth the circumstances by which a poor person has incurred loss, as by fire, the death of a horse, cow etc. Such a one takes the *brief* about to collect money for his indemnification.' Elworthy quotes a vernacular comment on the word from Somerset, which has a very authentic ring: "Tes a sight aisier for to run about wi' a brief 'n tes to work.' Certainly, the event was never forgotten; particularly if the family showed signs of *hubris* thereafter: 'Giddaway, I mind, one time, when they comed round wi' the brief for he!'

BRYANITES

This is not, strictly, a dialect word. It is in the *OED* but not the *EDD,* though it is very much a word of the westcountry. The Bryanites, or Bible Christians, were (I quote the *OED*) 'a Protestant sect founded in 1815 by William O.Bryan, a Wesleyan preacher in Cornwall; chiefly in the South West of England'. The term Bryanite is rare now, and even in its hey-day in early Victorian times it tended to have opprobrious overtones, with suggestions of a bucolic, hayseed madness about it: 'the fiery Bryanites', or 'the mad Bryanites' were common descriptions. The alternative name survived longer, however, and there are still 'wayside Bethels' in Devon and Cornwall which have rather misleading dates like B.C. 1859 on the foundation stone; B.C. standing for Bible Christian.

The name Bible Christian was not given without good reason. The early Bryanites were saturated in the Bible; so much so that the early minutes are in places almost unintelligible to those who have no acquaintance with the Authorised Version.

Q. Who has died this year?
A. Margaret Adams: who for a while laboured in the vineyard of the Lord with much diligence, zeal and success; having had many seals to her ministry and souls for her hire. She conducted herself as a Mother in Israel . . . beloved and esteemed in the Church; and owned by God as His messenger.

A winning personality, and an eloquent preacher, O.Bryan was nevertheless, as his friend and co-religionist, James Thorne, put it, 'a better pioneer than an organiser'; he had about him more than a dash of histrionic instability which led him to make grandiose but embarrassing gestures. From his conversion, as a boy, at a preaching service in the farmhouse at Bokiddick, to his leaving the sect he had founded at the 1828 Shebbear Conference with the words, 'Cursed shalt thou be in the city, and cursed shalt thou be in the field' (Deuteronomy 28: 16), his was a stormy career; it was probably as well for the sect that the leadership passed from this volatile Cornishman to more sagacious Devonians like Thorne.

The Cornishman is by nature a villager; he even prefers, if possible, a special place smaller than a nucleated village. This was the great appeal of O.Bryan's movement: an intensely local religion, with local preachers and a chapel, ideally, in every hamlet. If the interest was divided between two or three localities, there was always the Biblical precedent of casting lots: 'After preaching, our preacher wrote three lots – for Twelveheads, Tippett's Stemps, and Cross Lanes . . . When they drew lots the lot came for Cross Lanes to be the place for the chapel.' Building a chapel required a great effort, as building and restoring the parish churches had done in that other great era of church-building in Cornwall, the fifteenth century; but the result was there for all to see. It was, to use a word with most powerful associations in the South West, the *cause*: 'How's your little cause over to Nanstallon?' – such was the frequent phrase.

It is extraordinary that this religious movement, which

spread throughout the West of England, the Scillies and 'the Norman Isles' (Channel Islands) to various towns in the east and north, to Canada, Australia, New Zealand and China, eventually to reassociate with the Wesleyan Methodists in 1907, should have emanated from the little village of Luxulyan. Only rarely can the backwoods have been so elevated; but the towns, of course, had nearly all been evangelised by Wesley in the previous century. The Bryanite achievement was a sort of mopping-up operation for rural communities. First in the early minutes comes Luxulyan district, incorporating Penzance, Truro, Falmouth etc. Sixth is London, including Chatham, Brighton etc – a reasonable priority, since the Luxulyan circuit had 968 Bible Christians, whereas London had only 341! As befitted its status as a metropolitan, Luxulyan had three Bryanite chapels within the parish, in addition to Gunwen, which had been built by O.Bryan but which the Wesleyans had wrested from him.

In 1906, as a sort of swansong before final amalgamation with the Wesleyans in the next year, a most interesting book was published by W. S. Michell: *Brief Biographical Sketches of Bible Christian Ministers and Laymen.* The two volumes constitute both a testimonial to the past and an advertisement for the future. For the clergymen, especially, they must have represented a sort of clerical hiring fair. Nearly all the men photographed in it are products of the smaller rural chapels of the South West. The roll-call is mainly from villages and hamlets, some of them so small that they are known only to those with an intimate knowledge of local geography: Pensilva, Milton Damerel, Hicks Mill, Polskeys, Bosnieves, Harrowbarrow. From these and other small places, men of light and leading came forward. Often they were self-educated men, but many were trained at the Bryanite seminary, Shebbear College, which expanded from an unknown school into one of the principal means of further education (through its 'theological faculty') for rural Devon and Cornwall in the latter half of the nineteenth century.

When I was a boy, elderly people who recollected the time before 1907 always asked any promising schoolboy, 'What are 'ee going to be? A minister?' But the youth of my generation had different ideas.

CAP'N

This title is used in Cornish mining and china-clay areas for a manager or overseer. The word may have been introduced by German miners in the fifteenth century. Carew certainly knew the usage: 'The captain's office bindeth him to sort each workman his task, to see them apply their labour, to make timely provision for binding the work with frames of timber if need exact it, to place pumps for drawing off water, and to give such other directions.'

The 'Cap'n' was regarded with respect by the community, for he was a representative of a meritocracy. The difference between merited and inherited status is reflected in a curious fact of usage. It is possible, and indeed quite common, to address someone as either 'Cap'n' or 'Squire' in dialect, even when neither title is official; but I have noticed that 'Cap'n' is never used ironically, but is a mark of genuine respect for leadership, whereas 'Squire' often accompanies a sarcastic remark. John Pearce recalls the following conversation, referring to a distinguished officer of World War I:

'Where was W—— Cap'n to?'
'He wasn't a proper Cap'n. B'lieve he was only in the Navy!'

It was, and perhaps still is, usual to refer to the wives of clay-captains as 'Mrs Cap'n' and one woman I knew insisted on this: 'My name isn't Mrs Tremayne, dear; 'tis Mrs Cap'n Tremayne.'

'CHIELD'

Chaucer pronounced *child* to rhyme with standard English *healed,* and so they still do in the South West. The word tends to mean an infant in arms or a toddler, though as a vocative it can be used by any older speaker to any younger female: 'Please yourself, chield; you'm old enough to know your own mind now.' More specifically, the word can be used of any baby girl, as it was in the time of Shakespeare, who, according to the *OED,* never used the expression 'my child' of or to a son, but only with daughters. 'Is it a boy or a child?' is usage in the West of England, from Shropshire to Cornwall, according to the *EDD.* Another fairly common phrase is 'no chick nor child', said, at times enviously, of childless people by those whose quiver is too full of arrows.

This use of the vowel instead of the modern diphthong, indicated by the spelling *chield,* is some five hundred years behind the development of standard English. There are some parallels in a few westcountry place-names. We can contrast the pronunciation of St Ive, near Callington, as St *Eve,* with the pronunciation of the more famous St Ives; the former place is remote enough to have escaped the change of sound. There is also the village of Ide, near Exeter, which is pronounced to rhyme with *bead,* rather than with *bide.*

CHUFFED

We must face the sad fact that these days the population of Devon and Cornwall is in some places less than fifty per cent native. We shall not therefore be surprised if many dialect words are lost, or even overlaid by meanings from elsewhere.

The process is well shown by what has happened to the word *chuff.* Ask any Devonian or Cornish speaker over the age of fifty, and the chances are that he will tell you that this word means 'ill-tempered, cross, sulky': 'I could see he was brave 'n chuff.' The younger generation, however, will probably tell you that *chuff* (or *chuffed*) means 'pleased, elated': 'He likes the job and is quite chuffed about it.' This last is not a westcountry, but a Midlands and northcountry meaning of the word. The first volume of the new supplement to the *OED,* issued in 1972, indicates the present state of affairs well. Under *chuffed* there are four illustrative quotations in the sense of 'pleased' (1957–67) and only two in the sense of 'displeased' (1960 and 1964).

Which things, doubtless, are an allegory. The northern dialects, it seems, will be the last to die out. They have already given standard English words like *gormless* and *gawp*, and ITV's 'Coronation Street' has familiarised the whole South West with *jam-butties* and exclamations like 'Are they heck as like!' Taught by the Lancashire gardening expert Bill Sowerbutts, many people elsewhere than in the North of England may now call a watering-can a *degging-can*, or speak of vigour or strength in a plant as *bant*, though these were originally northern dialect terms. It is quite likely that the general northern dialectal adjective to describe sticky substances – *clarty* – will replace south-western ones like *clidgy*, *clibby* and *clisty*. A high-spirited person, a practical joker or a 'live wire', may still be characterised by the Cornish dialect noun a *buster*, but he is more likely to be called by some more urban and less local expression such as a *card* (shades of Arnold Bennett), a *caution* or a *cough-drop*.

Nevertheless, there are still one or two shibboleths of language, as between the westcountry and other areas. Thus a sentence like Ena Sharples's, *'Are them* fancies fresh?' (referring, of course, to fancy cakes) would in Devon and Cornwall dialect have the variant, *'Be they* fancies fresh?'

CITY

When Richard Carew of Antony, the Elizabethan topographer, visited my native village of Roche, he seems, like many tourists of today, not to have stopped for long:

> After we have quitted Restormel, Roche becomes our next place of sojourn, though hardly inviting with promise of any better entertainment than the name carrieth written in his forehead, to wit, a huge high, and steep rock seated in a plain, girded on either side with (as it were) two substitutes, and meritorious (no doubt) for the hermit who dwelt on the top thereof, were it but in regard of such an uneasy climbing to his cell and chapel, a part of whose natural wall is wrought out of the rock itself . . . From hence ascending easily the space of a mile, you shall have won the top of the Cornish archbeacon Hainborough, which (as little to great) may for prospect compare with Rama in Palestine . . . for if the weather's darkness bound not your eyesight, within his ordi-

35

nary extent you shall therein plainly discern, to the Eastward, a great part of Devon, to the West very near the Land's End, to the North and South, the ocean and sundry islands scattered therein; wherethrough it also passeth for a wonder.

Carew, like most Cornishmen, has his own sense of proportion. I remember once receiving a comic picture postcard in which Cornwall was seen as a large mainland, to which the smaller peninsula of Britain was attached. 'The centre of the county is reported to be a hole in a field at Probus', writes Miss Courtney, and, in the same self-centred vein, others have considered that the most central parish is Lanivet.

So Carew, always readable as he is, should not be checked with a slide-rule. 'Ascending easily the space of a mile' from Roche Rock will, in fact, get you no nearer 'Hainborough' than Higher Trezaise, 'hardly inviting with promise of any better entertainment' than, perhaps, a few *whorts* (whortle-berries, pronounced as *hurts*) in late July. There is still 'a brave little step' (a phrase to be wary of) before Hensbarrow, as it is now called. As for Hensbarrow beacon itself – what we can see of it for mounds of china-clay waste – well, perhaps Mount Rama is slightly larger, but we do not measure these things ('as little to great') with ordinary yardsticks.

Other instances of slight distortion of measurement west of the Tamar, are noted by that most observant Victorian folklorist and dialectician, Miss Courtney:

Every stream in Cornwall, however small, is called a river (pronounced *revvur*).

I asked an old woman three or four years ago, who lived not far from the little village of Gwithian, where I could get something I wanted; and she told me 'In the city.'

It was usual to parade down through one's village on a Saturday night, often nominally with the excuse of getting the wireless accumulator charged, but actually to see 'the world'. On returning, one would be asked, 'Well, who did you see in the city?'

Curiously, in one field of vocabulary there is an opposite, belittling tendency. A blow, in fighting, is often a *poke*, a *pat*

36

or a *dab*. 'Next time I shall pat at 'un', is a more formidable threat than it sounds, and there is an old rhyme from the Penzance area, expressing characteristic local animosity:

> Penzance boys up in a tree,
> Looking as wisht as wisht can be.
> Newlyn 'buccas', strong as oak,
> Knocking 'em down at every poke.

CLICKY

Many English words have special meanings in the South West. *Clubbish,* for instance, far from suggesting gregariousness or friendliness, means 'bullying' or 'brutal': 'Don't 'ee be so clubbish with your little sister!' This meaning was found in more standard English in former centuries. Sir Thomas North, the Elizabethan translator of Plutarch, described a tyrant as 'a mean man, and of a clubbish nature'. Dialectally, the adjective *sparky* has not much to do with sparks, but is used of cattle that are mottled in colour – especially brown mottled white: 'How much for your sparky cow, missus?' I remember a woman being asked as she was driving her bullocks to their meadow. Sarah Hewett has this sentence, which perhaps only a Devonian can paraphrase accurately: 'Vather went to Holsery Fair and buyed dree sparky cows.' *Clicky* in the Cornish dialect has no connection with machinery or gadgets; it is from a Celtic root meaning 'left-handed', inviting comparison with Cornish *cledhek* (left handed). A batsman's opponent is described in the *EDD* as 'a difficult man – he can bowl right-handed or clicky'.

Another word which, like *clicky,* has a special meaning in the South West, is *grainy,* which occurs in the sense of 'haughty', 'over-refined'. Here, however, there is a connection to be seen. Scarlet grain dye (often, in fact, from an insect, not from part of a plant) was used in the colouring of very fine cloth, giving rise to expressions like 'dyed in grain', used originally of material dyed scarlet, then of any fast colour and eventually of firmly held or refined ideas. We can discern an interesting half-way meaning in the imperfectly recorded dialect use of *grain* to assert standards of laundry: 'a wisht poor grain' is a phrase still in use in mid-Cornwall to describe the kind of whiteness now stigmatised as having been produced by Brand X washing powders. It is interesting that the English word seems to have been imported into Welsh dialects in precisely the same kind of context. In one of Welsh author Kate Roberts's short stories the phrase occurs: 'Yr oedd y fath *raen* ar ei dillad glân', ie 'There was such a *grain* on her clean clothes' (allow for the loss of the 'g' by initial mutation).

CLOAM

This word is of Anglo-Saxon rather than Celtic derivation. *Cloam,* from Old English *clam* (earthenware, clay), means what in the North is called *pot*. A *pot egg,* placed in a nesting-box to encourage hens to lay, is known in the westcountry as a *cloam egg,* and the northern phrase – now heard a great deal from 'imports' – 'washing the pots' for 'washing dishes', still causes some amusement in the West, where *pots* means 'chamber-pots'. A person lacking in solidity or worth is said to be 'like an old cloam cat, hollow to the toes'. In a footnote to his novel *The Astonishing History of Troy Town* Q tells us that in 'Troy' (Fowey), drinking was euphemistically called 'emptying cloam'.

A frequent collocation used to be *cloam oven*. I quote A. K. Hamilton-Jenkin's *Cornish Homes and Customs*:

> In the central and eastern parts of the county . . . the open hearths (were) generally provided with a 'cloam' or earthenware oven, built into their sides. These ovens are square in shape, with a slightly domed top . . . Before cooking, a fire of furze, chaff, or bruss is kindled within the oven, and allowed to burn until the latter has been heated to the proper temperature. The embers are then swept out with a little broom or rag called a 'malkin', after which the food is placed inside, the earthenware dome of the oven 'put home', and the contents left to cook in the gradually diminishing heat.

'Like the end of a house' is a regular description of a stout, and especially a pregnant woman, but the number of cottages still to be seen which retain the bellying chimney-end, indicating that formerly there was an open hearth with a cloam oven inside, is now fast diminishing.

The traditional use of furze-bushes (*vuzz*) to heat the cloam oven has given rise to one amusing turn of phrase for someone who is half-witted or, in the dialect expression, *not 'zackly* (exactly): 'He'll bear a bush or two more' means, in effect, that he is only half-baked, or that, in another phrase which may recall the cloam oven, he was 'put in with the bread and took out with the cake'.

CLUNK

'He's chucken . . . Slap 'en, Calvin, quick! For 'tis clunk or stuffle, an' no time to lose.' I wonder how long this splendid sentence from Q's lengthy short-story 'The Three Ships' will continue to be understood. *Clunk or stuffle* means 'swallow or stifle'. To the trick question 'Do you know how the St Issey people eat junket?' the traditional answer was 'They put it in their mouth and clunk it'. *Clunk* is doubtless a Celtic Cornish word, probably from Cornish *collenky* 'to swallow down'. In one of Kate Roberts's best-known stories, 'Pryfocio', a woman makes a remark drinking a 'gulp' of tea as she does so: 'gan yfed *llwnc o dê*'. Despite the spelling, this expression is closely related to 'a clunk of tay', as one might say in the Cornish dialect. A joke question sometimes asked because of its incomprehensibility to those not deeply versed in dialect is, 'Have 'ee ever seen a mollard clunk a gay?', that is, 'Have you ever seen a drake swallow a potsherd?' One's *clunker* is one's windpipe: 'I got a crumb hanged up in me clunker' was recorded in Altarnun in the 1950s.

COOSE

The frisken chaps did skip about
An' coose the maidens in and out.

This authentically westcountry, if rather uncharacteristically pedestrian, couplet is by William Barnes of Dorset. Grammatically, *coose* is perhaps the most versatile word in the dialects of the South West. It can be a noun, a verb, an adjective or an adverb, and means so many things that a stranger may well be puzzled. The reason is that this overworked word can, dialectally, be a variant of two standard English words of the same sound but different spelling, origin and meaning – *coarse* and *course*. Thus a coarse woman is said to be *coose;* but we also *coose* people when we chase them, and we can, or could as children, play 'a game of coose'. We can also run up a hill *some coose,* meaning, 'at a great rate', or 'go our own coose', ie 'at our own pace'.

The phrase *some coose* illustrates the adverbial use of *some,* still very common: 'She's some good maid to work.' As used here, *some* is rather like the normal adverb of degree, *very,* but is not interchangeable with it because very needs an indefinite article, whereas some does not. The word some can also occur as an adjective with intensifying force; thus 'He got some money' can have two meanings – either, as in standard English, 'He has a certain amount of money', or, dialectally, 'He has a large fortune'. In speech, however, there is no possibility of confusion; if the dialect meaning is intended, some bears strong stress.

DAG

It is arguable that the word *axe* represents a deficiency in the English language. It covers anything from the two-handed instrument wielded so drastically by executioners on the heads of noble traitors, to a household tool for chopping wood. It is true that the *OED* recommends the word *hatchet* for such a comparatively pacific article, but I suspect that axe is the word chiefly used in English to cover most kinds of 'chopper'. After all, the axe with which Lizzie Borden gave her father forty whacks seems not to have been a 'two-handed engine'.

In Devon and Cornwall, however, there is no problem, because the word *dag* is used for anything smaller than a woodman's axe. A *dag* will also serve in its humble way as an executioner's weapon, for with a *dag* and some determination, a *stag* can be beheaded for Sunday dinner. Such a dinner would be of poultry, however, not of venison, for, except possibly on Exmoor, this is the first meaning of the word *stag* in the South West, viz, a cock, or, euphemistically speaking, a rooster. When I suggested in *The Western Morning News* that this meaning of *stag* was dying out, readers from East Cornwall and North Devon corrected me; the term, which probably originates in cockfighting, is still the only one that many farmers use. Canon Hammond relates that a school inspector was puzzled when, having asked a class to name what it was that recalled Peter to repentance after he had denied his Lord, he received the answer, 'A stag, sir.'

Apropos of *dag*, there is also a curious, and still very common, use of the word in Cornwall as a quite distinct defective verb; defective, because found in the present participle only. *Dagging* is an emphatic word meaning 'longing', 'eager': 'I could see he was *dagging* to know, but I never said.' Wright, in the *EDD*, connects this with the sense of 'a shooting or darting pain', but this is northern and Midlands, not southwestern usage, and I am not convinced.

DIDO

Embedded in Q's *Troy Town* is the amusing incidental tale of lawyer Mennear and the glass eye. His glass eye gave the lawyer what Q calls a 'janjansy kind of look'. Defining this (now obsolete) word as 'two-faced', Q asks in a footnote whether the word may not be derived from Janus, the Roman god and doorkeeper of heaven, noted for facing both ways. It is difficult to account for such knowledge of the classics in dialect speakers; just as it is difficult to see the connection, which has been suggested, between the still commonly heard phrase 'kicking up a dido', ie a 'row' or a 'shindy', and Dido, mythical queen of Carthage – even though she did kick up a 'purdy dido' when Æneas deserted her.

The older generation still speak of *keeping up,* rather than *kicking up,* a *dido,* and this is of interest because there are similar Welsh phrases for 'to make a noise' – *cadw stwr, cadw swn* and *cadw twrw* – and a similar use of *keep* also occurs in the English dialect of Pembrokeshire.

The Welsh word *stwr* is clearly an English loan, comparable with the widespread dialect word *stour* or *stewer,* meaning, in the South West, either a cloud of dust or, metaphorically, a commotion or a row: 'never happier than when she's kicking up a stewer'.

DOIT

Shakespeare enjoyed laughing at the foibles of his fellow-countrymen. In *The Tempest* Trinculo comments on the Englishman's tendency to be curious rather than generous:

> Were I in England now (as once I was) and had but this fish painted . . . Any strange beast there makes a man: when they will not give a doit to relieve a lame beggar, they will lay out ten to see a dead Indian.

A *doit* was a small coin, Dutch in origin, the value of half an English farthing. In the South West, and with a dialectal pronunciation that rhymes with *bite,* the word has developed to mean a person of very small stature: 'He's such a little doit.'

Words spelt with *oi* and *oy* are not English in origin, but mostly loans from French (*boil, join*) or, as in the case of *doit,* from Dutch. The westcountry pronunciation of *doit* was common with all *oi* words in earlier English, as is confirmed by the rhymes of eighteenth-century hymn-writers like Charles Wesley:

> Come, let us use the grace *divine*
> And all, with one accord,
> In a perpetual convenant *join*
> Ourselves to Christ the Lord.

It is interesting also that Wesley's line 'Hell is *nigh* but God is nigher' seems less old-fashioned in the West than elsewhere, since the word *nigh* is there an everyday occurrence, not a poeticism.

DOWNSER

'Then where are the moors?'
'The moors, missie? Why here be the moors. There's . . .

42

Nethermoor, and there's Withymoor, and right away off there is Sedgemoor.'

'Oh, but I do not call these moors at all. This is quite a fraud. A moor ought to be covered with heather and rough ponies. I call these fens.'

This conversation, between a Somersetshire man and someone who is obviously not a native, occurs in a Victorian novel, *Misterton's Mistake,* by Walter Raymond. The remark is applicable to the whole of the South West, where upland hill-country, despite names like Exmoor, Dartmoor and Bodmin Moor, is more likely to be called *downs* than moors, and what is contemptuously referred to by the farmer as 'a little moory piece' is probably a low-lying, marshy area. It is only by making this distinction between *downs* and *moors* that we can make sense of the weather-rhyme:

> Mist on the hill
> Brings water to the mill.
> Mist on the moor
> Brings sunshine to your door.

As Professor Charles Thomas notes, *moor* often had this meaning in the standard language down to the eighteenth century. It is implicit in these lines from Spenser, for example:

> Therto the frogs, bred in the slimie scouring
> Of the moist moores, their jarring voices bent.

The use of the word *downs* for the kind of country defined by Professor Thomas as 'high and plateau country with predominantly dry conditions and heath or bracken cover' yields the noun *downser,* either for a bullock grazed on the downs (West Cornwall) or for a rough person, reared in what sometimes used to be called the *higher quarter,* ie the area above the tree-line.

A more local synonym for *downser* in mid-Cornwall is *Carslaker.* Carslake has ceased to exist; contrary to the scriptural dictum that 'a city set on a hill cannot be hid', it is being buried by a mound of china-clay waste. Until recently, situated 1,000ft above sea level, near Hensbarrow, it was the most prominent hamlet in the middle of the county. Whatever viewpoint you took, from Helman Tor near Bodmin, from out to sea in St Austell bay, or from the hills above Fowey, Carslake was a row of clay-workers' houses that stood out like teeth on the horizon.

Also not far from Hensbarrow was Greensplat; but Greensplat was a different case. For one thing there was a chapel, whereas the ultimate count in the indictment against Carslakers was that 'they didn't know Sundays from Mondays'. Thirty years ago, along with others, I performed at various concerts at Greensplat chapel. 'Purdy!' they used to shout when the entertainment pleased them, 'Purdy!', and they would clap and stamp their feet in approval. (Stamping of feet was frowned on in chapels below the tree-line.) Afterwards there would be hot pasties and jelly served on the hymn-book ledges, for the money did not run to a Sunday school-room at Greensplat.

The *plat* of Greensplat, is a dialect word in itself. A *plat*, in smallholding contexts, is a small piece of green near a dwelling-house, suitable for a few geese, a clothes-line etc. In tin-mining, it is an open space near a mine-shaft. According to Mrs Kathleen Hawke, *plat* is also West Cornwall dialect for 'a platform on a stairs' ie a spacious turn in a staircase where the stairs do not ascend in a single flight. Those who know the farmhouses of the South West will instantly recognise what she means by the latter. Such houses, spacious, with roomy staircases, are mostly 100 years old and more; built idiosyncratically, but well, by local builders, they are now described by house-agents as 'houses of character'. Often such houses, like Mr Melbury's in Hardy's Little Hintock (*The Woodlanders*), have an official entrance and garden-front not much used for everyday access, and, as with the house of the Idens in *Amaryllis at the Fair*, the way through to the various rooms is known as the *passage*, even though this may be three times the size of the 'halls' and 'vestibules' of suburbia.

DOXY

In the South West the word *doxy* both changes from a noun to an adjective, and sheds its undesirable overtones. It was a regular eighteenth-century word for a low wench or a prostitute, and in standard English it still calls up suggestions of John Gay's *The Beggar's Opera*: 'Thus I stand like a Turk with his doxies around.' But in Devon and Cornwall *doxy*, when used of women, is a compliment, meaning 'dainty' or 'petite': 'He do belong going with a party down Nanstallon; doxy little piece.' The *EDD* has a nice Devon quotation from Mrs Hewett: 'Idden her a doxy duck, in thickee there new bonnet?' Doxiness in later life, however, can lead to dumpiness, and there is a less complimentary epithet for the short middle-aged or elderly lady whose shape approaches the spherical:

> A *Dolly 'pon truckles* (ie small wheels, castors)
> All flesh and no knuckles.

'DRECKLY'

People in the South West are sometimes accused of being lazy; sometimes by those who, for one reason or another, have retired to the area, unable to stand the pace they have created for themselves in the Midlands or the North. There is certainly one manifestation of a tendency to procrastinate, or as it is put in the West, of considering that 'there's another day 'morrow 'idn touched yet'; this is that the word *directly* in Devon and Cornwall has gone the way of standard English *presently,* and no longer means 'immediately' but 'in a minute or two'. The *EDD* quotes, from the Hartland area of Devon: 'I'll come dreckly; I must finish what I'm 'bout first.'

DUMMETS

This prosaic sounding word is the equivalent of standard English *twilight,* a word whose origin, incidentally, is recalled in the dialect phrase 'between the two lights'. It was the Scots who retained the Old English word *glomung,* which seems, however, to have come back into standard English as *gloaming,* partly through Burns. To compare *gloaming* and *dummets* is to reveal a difference between northern and south-western dialects. In general, while there is much humour in the dialects of the South West, there is little romance. It is the inconvenient, and not the romantic, side of twilight that is stressed in *dummets,* as also in *blind man's holiday,* used when the light is no longer good enough to work by. Unlike the Scots, who have always understood publicity and how to exploit the real, if sometimes tenuous, connection between poetry and the cash-register, westcountrymen have often been ready to undersell their best assets with a cynical shrug of the shoulders. How well Thomas Hardy understood all this! The passage in *The Mayor of Casterbridge* where Farfrae sings his romantic Scots ballads to shrewd Dorset comments, penetrates deeply into regional differences:

> 'Danged if our country down here is worth singing about like that!' continued the glazier, as the Scotchman again melodised with a dying fall, "My ain countree!" 'What did ye come away from yer ain country for, young maister, if ye be so wownded about it? Be dazed, if I loved my country half as well as the young feller do, I'd live by claining out my neighbour's pigsties afore I'd go away!'

Two south-western phrases which *do* reveal that the imagination is engaged at a deeper level are the intensive 'to the truth of music', as in 'She lectured him to the truth of music', and the expression, found in several Victorian glossaries but now, I fear, lost, *in the vestries,* used of an infant smiling in his sleep.

ELLY

It is surprising what significant scraps of dialect can be rescued, even at this late date, from oblivion. In 1936 a contributor to the magazine *Old Cornwall* quoted an admonition to a lazy person, often formerly heard: 'You don't elly to do nothen', that is , 'You make no effort or purposeful attempt to do anything'. The then editor, R. Morton Nance, called for corroboration, but none seems to have been forthcoming in later volumes. Nevertheless, there is no doubt about the existence of this word, though it is in no glossary so far as I know. I can confirm its use by my grandmother, who quoted it as a word that had grown uncommon in her lifetime. The phrase she illustrated its use with was almost identical: 'He won't elly to do anything.'

Nance suggested a derivation from OE *elnian*, 'to strengthen, hearten, support', a word that is not in the *EDD* and which died out in the thirteenth century according to the *OED*. I doubt this very much. It corresponds much more closely in meaning to the Northern and Scottish dialect verb *ettle*. In a sentence such as Wright quotes from Ayrshire, 'After a long, faithful, and undaunted effort . . . she saw that all her ettling was of no avail', the word clearly has a similar meaning to south-western *elly*. *Ettle*, however, is normally taken to be from Old Norse, hence the reason for its surviving in the dialects of the North only. Could there have been an unrecorded, but related word in Old English, which then turns up in the South West as *elly*?

ENT

Ent, meaning 'to empty or pour' as in 'enting down with rain', is still occasionally heard. A Truro correspondent remembers being sent to buy a teapot with the admonition, 'and see he got a good ent to 'un'; that is, of course, a good 'pour'. Canon Hammond related that a Gwennap man refused to contribute to Queen Victoria's Golden Jubilee on the grounds that the Queen had too many over-paid servants: 'There's the Lord Chamberlain . . . 'e do draw £5,000 a year . . . and what do 'a do for it? Only make the beds, ent a few slops and that sort of thing!'

EVIL

When we hear, as we frequently do in the South West, a long-handled four-pronged dung-fork called an *evil,* the temptation is to connect the word with the devil's pitch-fork. This would be a faulty association. The Old English word for a fork is

47

eaful, a quite separate word which is the ancestor both of the more widespread *evil* in this sense of 'dung-fork', and of the East Cornwall *yule.* An *evil* can also be called a *prong,* but so could a dinner-fork until recently. A hay-fork, in Cornwall, is normally called a *pike,* which has more military overtones in earlier standard English. Another case of beating swords into ploughshares and spears into pruning hooks is the word *vizgy* or *bizgy,* still occasionally heard in the dialects of Devon and Cornwall for a 'twybill' or two-headed pick (there is some variation, but one blade could be at right angles to the other); a *vizgy* (French *bisaigue,* Latin *bisacutus*) was formerly a two-edged weapon of war.

The use of *evil* for a manure fork is a good example of things in dialect being other than they seem. The opposite of evil in standard English is goodness, but in dialect *goodness* can mean 'cooking-fat': 'Put plenty of goodness in that pastry.' *Anguish,* too, is not an abstract word for distress or suffering, but a concrete one meaning 'inflammation': 'That is the anguish coming out' is said when an eye that has been inflamed starts to water. *Order* can mean 'disorder, confusion', as in 'There was some order over to the dance last night', ie a rumpus or a row. In dialect, for a woman to be called 'a pretty beauty' is, contrary to appearances, no compliment; it means she has no morals whatever!

In mid-Cornwall and farther west it is usual to lift potatoes etc from the garden with a long-handled fork. It is also common practice, perhaps because of the mining and clay-work tradition, to dig the ground not with a short-handled spade, but a shovel with a long *bowed* hilt. Thus the SED, seeking the word for the shaft of a spade, found that in much of Cornwall the article was not known, and they had to be content with shovel-hilt.

FALLY

On the whole, I think we may take it that it is much pleasanter to write about folk-life than to earn your living by participating. When I am tempted to sentimentalise over old 'folkways' and bygone customs, I moderate my nostalgia with the memory of 'binding wheels' in my father's black-smith's shop. How bad-tempered and unspeakable 'binding wheels' made everybody! All the doors would be shut, even on a hot day, with both lots of bellows going to keep the rim, covered with ashes, hot all round; then came the quick opening of the doors and the men would rush out with the white-hot *bind* or 'rim' to the wooden cart-wheel waiting on its stone platform. My job was getting buckets of water ready and pouring it as directed – 'Spoke-head!' 'Middle of the vally!' – so that the iron tyre or *bind* (known as a *bend* in West Cornwall) suddenly cooled and shrank into the wood.

What was this word *vally* or *fally*? I knew where to throw the water at least: on the section of the rim between the spokes. The word is really a mid-Cornwall variant of *felly* or *felloe,* and the *vallies* are the curved segments of the wooden rim which, joined together, form the wheel.

Was our pronunciation *vally* popular or folk etymology, then, by association with the commoner word *valley*? I think not, for folk are not that simple-minded. Moreover, Shakes-peare (from the western half of England, after all) had something very near this form in *Hamlet* (I quote from the First Folio):

> Out, out, thou Strumpet – Fortune! all you Gods . . .
> Breake all the Spokes and Fallies from her wheele
> And boule the round Nave downe the hill of Heauen.

In different dialects, there are at least a dozen varieties of this word.

FARDEL

'(The Turks) one and all, bag and baggage, shall, I hope, clear out from the province they have desolated and profaned.' That was what Mr Gladstone said, on 7 May 1877, on the occasion of the Bulgarian atrocities. In my boyhood, Mr Glad-stone was still a name to conjure with. We had his picture on a tea-caddy, and some of my contemporaries in the 1930s were still being christened Ewart, but all the same, we did not copy Mr Gladstone's phrase, 'bag and baggage'. We had our own vituperative way of dismissing people: 'I told 'un to clear out, pack and vardel!' The word, stemming from French *fardeau*, recalls, despite the difference of register, one of the great 'set pieces' of English literature – the 'To be or not to be' soliloquy of *Hamlet*:

> Who would fardels bear,
> To grunt and sweat under a weary life,
> But that the dread of something after death –
> That undiscovered country from whose bourn
> No traveller returns – puzzles the will,
> And makes us rather bear those ills we have
> Than fly to others that we know not of.

The element of 'pack, baggage, burden' is common to both contexts.

The Reverend Baring-Gould quotes an anecdote of Antony Payne, the 7ft 2in Cornish giant, servant of Sir Basil Greville of Stowe, in the parish of Kilkhampton. Payne was ordered, one Christmas Eve, to hurry up a dilatory boy, who had been sent out with a donkey to bring wood for the fire. Shortly afterwards the giant came back, bearing the loaded animal on his shoulders and calling out, 'Ass and fardel! Ass and fardel for my lady's Yule!'

How did one describe stale news before Queen Anne died? The answer was, if we are to believe Swift's *Polite Conversations,* 'Queen Elizabeth's dead'. But again, as with 'bag and baggage', there is a south-western equivalent, possibly peculiar to East Cornwall. Writing from London on 10 September 1793 to his sister Elizabeth in Bodmin, William Clift says: 'I receiv'd a letter from Brother John since I received your first in which he told me (*ropers news*) that you and him had had a difference.' 'Roper's news, hang the crier' is the full expression, according to the Victorian glossaries, but it is not a form that I have heard.

FERNAIGUE

Generally, the far South West, like other areas broadly designated 'the Celtic fringe', has always been rather less class-conscious than many other parts of Britain. Nevertheless, there were distinctions; they appear, for instance, in card-games, where refinement, or lack of it, always shows. Taking a point from Dickens's *Great Expectations*, Q embroiders on it in *The Astonishing History of Troy Town*: 'When Mr Simpson had spoken of the 'Jack of Oaks' (meaning the knave of clubs), or had said fainaiguing (where others said revoking), we had pretended not to notice it.' *Fernaiguing* (Q's is an etymological spelling which does not indicate the pronunciation well), besides meaning 'to revoke at cards', has the more general sense of 'to break an agreement'– to *run word*, as the westcountry idiom goes. The *EDD* quotes from Somerset for an instance of the latter phrase: 'I bought Farmer Snow's wheat in vower shillings a bushel an' took the sample; but 'vore 'twas drashed, 'twas better worth, and he urn'd word.' Note that the past tense of *run word* is rendered *urn'd word* or (always in Cornwall and usually now, no doubt, in Devon and Somerset too) the unmetathesised *runn'd*. I am sure that, rather than say *ran word*, people will adopt a more standard English expression like 'broke his word'. Standard grammar kills dialect idiom.

Another card-playing word used in the South West, but not found in the *EDD* and perhaps not dialect at all, even though it is not heard elsewhere, is *euchred*, from the allegedly American card-game of *euchre*. It means 'beaten', 'non-plussed', or, to use a dialect synonym, *fitchered*. *Fitchered*, however, carries suggestions of work, not play, for according to the glossaries, it is 'used in mining when some difficulty occurs in boring a hole for blasting'. Like some other technical terms, it also occurs more widely. Thus a mechanic mending a car may well be *fitchered*, temporarily. Perhaps he has lost one of those nameless small parts: 'I've lost that little *udjia* or *udjiack*,' he might say; or, expanding without clarifying (rather as standard *thingummy* extends to *thingummibob*), he might add, 'that little *udjiackapiffy*'. *Udjiack*, too, is a technical term, but in this instance from shipbuilding: 'a movable chock used in fitting the planks of a boat' is R. Morton Nance's definition, from his *Glossary of Cornish Sea-words*.

FIGGY HOBBAN

'Her dinner was of saffron cake or a figgy hobban (a lump of dough with a handful of figs, as they call raisins, stuck in the middle of it and baked).' So a Cornish *bal-maiden* (woman surface worker at a mine) is described in a Victorian short story. *Hobban* or *hoggan,* a 'pastry-cake', is probably a Celtic Cornish derivation from Cornish *hogen.* The alternative form yields *hoggy* as in *tatie-hoggy,* another name, in some areas, for a pasty.

If *figs* means 'raisins', what is the word used for standard English figs, those fruits which, in the allegedly Mediterranean climate of the far West, can sometimes be grown and bear fruit out of doors? The answer is *broad figs.*

Two other apparent redundancies of the south-western dialects are *lamb-mint* where standard English makes do with *mint,* and *butcher's meat* for *meat.* The last phrase, however, is not really redundant, being a necessary distinction between home-cured meat and that obtained from the butcher. The phrase occurred widely in English literature down to Victorian times and was common in Trollope's novels, for example. *Butcher's meat* would be the most expensive item in the farm-labourer's budget. No doubt it was the scarcity of meat that gave rise to the jocular phrase 'taties and point', meaning, or so it was explained to me, 'Potatoes and point to the meat, to make sure nobody don't miss it.' It is not surprising to encounter the phrase in many British dialects, but it is curious to find Elworthy, in *The Dialect of West Somerset,* citing a similar idea from the Upper Punjab: 'A miser protests against another wasting his ghee by dipping his bread in it, when by hanging up the ghee out of reach on a nail, pointing the bread at it, and making believe very much, he might enjoy the ghee in imagination and save it in fact.'

FITTY

When we encounter the word *proper,* used so widely in the South West of any kind of excellence or thoroughness, we may recall the earlier English of the King James Bible (Hebrews 11:23): 'By faith Moses, when he was born, was hid three months of his parents, because they saw he was a proper child.' The accolade of approval is to be described as 'a proper chap', and in Devon and Cornwall it is quite possible to reply to an inquiry after one's welfare with this single word:

'How are 'ee then?'
'Proper.'

The adverb *properly* is also common. An angry person can be said to be 'properly hurried'; a vindictive one, 'properly ghastly'. Strangely, this meaning of *ghastly* has never been recorded, so far as I know, although it is very common in mid-Cornwall. The use of *hurried*, however, in the sense of 'agitated, vexed, angry', is more widespread, being common in earlier English down to Victorian times. In Mrs Gaskell's *North and South* are the words, 'Mrs Hale was hurried', where *hurried* clearly has the now dialectal meaning of 'annoyed'.

An alternative to *properly hurried* might be *fitty hurried* or *vitty hurried*. The spelling *vitty* gives a better idea of the pronunciation (except in West Cornwall), but *fitty* indicates the connection with *fit* and possibly, as the editors of the *OED* believed, with *feat*. Thus, to do a thing *fitty* can mean not only to do it in a fitting way, but also in a manner that amounts to a *feat*, an action showing dexterity and skill. 'Foot it featly here and there' is Ariel's direction to the dancing sprites in *The Tempest*. Something of all this has passed into the meaning of this common and expressive word, *fitty*.

Sometimes a synonymous word, but one with rather a different emphasis, is heard. This is *suant* (or, farther east, *zuant*), connected with French *suivre*, 'to follow', and comparable with a legal term like *pursuant*. Hence an implication of a smooth 'follow-through' to the finish, of an even or regular performance. 'This mower', I heard a Sidmouth man grumble, 'won't mow the lawn zuant.'

FLASKET

'What do you carry the washed clothes in when you put them on the line to dry?' the *SED* fieldworkers asked westcountry housewives a few years ago. In Devon and Cornwall, but not elsewhere in the South apparently, the answer is a *flasket*, although the dialecticians themselves may well have been puzzled at first by the additional information of one housewife from West Devon: 'A flasket; but 'course, 'tis really a maund.' A *maund* is a rough basket, its wicker-work of unpeeled osiers, of the kind used formerly, perhaps still, to send new potatoes to London. This thrifty soul is practising habits learnt in harder days, of contriving and making do. I can just imagine the *maun* (the 'd' is often silent) being put by: ''Twill come in handy for a flasket.' Yet today, only a few years after the *SED,* the old-fashioned wicker flasket is itself becoming a bygone, nearly all flaskets now being made of polythene. Words have various ways of dying out; I would suggest that the reason this one may cease to exist is that 'a plastic flasket' is a terrible tongue-twister.

In *The Western Morning News* I originally wrote that broccoli also was transplanted in *maunds,* but was corrected by Mrs Rose Tonkin of Truro. *Broccolaw* (a dialectal form from the Italian singular *broccolo,* probably) are sent to market in taller baskets of open-work construction which allow air to circulate and prevent them from *quailing,* ie 'going flabby', on their journey *upward.*

Another word which, like *maund,* omits the final consonant, is *scythe,* pronounced like *sigh* or *zigh.* 'If 'twas left to 'e,' someone remarked of an old-fashioned farmer, 'we'd still be cutting corn with a zye.' This absence of a final consonant is in obvious contrast with words like *liard,* where an extra 'd' appears: 'If a chield can talk before it can walk,' runs the proverb, ''tis going to be a liard.' Some carol-singers favoured the version, '*Wild* shepherds watched their flocks by night'. It is on this principle of an excrescent 'd' at the end of the word that we can explain the dialectal verb *sound,* as in 'sounding away with laughing', which is an alternative form of 'swoon'.

Yorkshire pudding, it is said, is served first in Yorkshire to take the edge off one's appetite and spare the meat. There was a word for such stop-gap food in Cornwall; it was a *foacer*: 'Woll 'ee have a foacer, chield?'

The minginess of some Cornish farmers, though doubtless excusable from the lean years through which farming has passed within living memory, is proverbial. Up and down the county various men acquired the reputation of being, in dialect phrases, *tight*, 'as near as the grave', or even, in extreme instances, 'ready to skin a turd to get the hide and tallow'. One man at Mousehole was said to 'come over queer' if his wife happened to bring out a slice of cake for the boy's *crowst*. He would call out: 'Drink drop tay, drink drop tay, boy; caake weean't fill 'ee!' The opposite of *near* is *givish*, a rather attractive formation that should be in standard English. The *EDD* is wrong to quote it from Warwickshire only.

Along with meanness went habits of cutting and contriving, of 'putting everything to the last', that have been more or less dropped in these more affluent times. In the old days, if a cloam cup was broken, or a *paddick* (a word for a small pitcher), the potsherds would be ground up on a stone with a hammer and fed to the fowls, to make stronger eggshells for improved laying. If a shovel of the old Cornish mining variety were worn out, it might still be sunk into the earth blade first and serve as a boot-scraper outside the farmhouse back-door. There are probably still boot-scrapers like this to be seen in the South West.

FORERIGHT, FORTHY

There is some variation in the meaning of these two words, but on the whole, while neither adjective is complimentary, the two are not confused in the South West. *Foreright* means 'tactless, awkward, blundering' – 'foreright as a 'oss (horse)' is the usual comparison. *Forthy*, which in Scotland can mean 'affable' or 'cheerful', generally applies only to women in Devon and Cornwall, and is difficult to define. Perhaps there is no exact synonym. Once, when I was searching for a word to characterise a very cheeky girl pupil for the purpose of writing a school report, a westcountry teacher made the very apposite, though not, unfortunately, very practical, suggestion, 'Why not write that she's forthy?' *Forthy* means (roughly) 'pert, cheeky, over-sexed': a typical remark from village gossips is, 'Forthy little thing! Hot as mustard! She'll come with her arse to the ground and wish her cake dough!'

FRAME

In the bloodthirsty world of the Old Testament, pronunciation could literally be a matter of life and death:

> Then Jephthah gathered together all the men of Gilead, and fought with Ephraim . . . And the Gileadites took the passages of Jordan before the Ephraimites; and it was so, that when those Ephraimites which were escaped said Let me go over, that the men of Gilead said unto him Art thou an Ephraimite? If he said, Nay; then said they unto him, Say now Shibboleth: and he said Sibboleth; for he could not frame to pronounce it right. Then they took him and slew him at the passages of Jordan. (Judges 12: 4–6)

'He could not frame to pronounce it right' – this use of *frame* in the sense 'to put oneself in a posture of doing something' or 'to set about a work in a promising manner' is now much more common in dialectal than standard English. To 'frame up' in the westcountry means 'to strike an attitude for fighting, to square one's fists in readiness'. *Framer* is a not uncomplimentary nickname, as Cornish nicknames go, for the sort of man who is prepared to tackle anything.

GLAZE

For some purposes of language – abstract reasoning, for example – dialect is a blunt instrument. But in other fields, perhaps those in which dialect speakers are especially qualified by their technology, but in many cases by chance, there may be a rich synonymy for finely differentiated meanings that can put the standard language in the shade. Consider, for instance, the cluster of verbs expressing the idea of 'looking' that occur in Cornwall. Besides the standard *look, stare* and so on, there is this quartet: to *geek,* to *glaze,* to *glow* and to *gunny.* Some were formerly in the standard language. Shakespeare, for instance, knew the curious blend of *gaze* and *glare,* as in the dialectal 'What be 'ee glazing at?' or 'glazing like a sticked pig'. As an omen for Julius Caesar's death, the conspirator Casca saw a lion near the Capitol 'who glaz'd upon me and went surly by'. The word is often printed as *glared* or *gazed* in modern editions, but no Cornishman would fail to understand the First Folio text.

To *glow* (rhyming with *how,* not with *know*) means 'to stare angrily, to glower', and Chaucer has it at the beginning of his translation of Boethius, where the Philosopher is confronted with the personification of a displeased Philosophy who 'glowede with cruwel eyen'. To *gunny* means to 'peer closely', perhaps short-sightedly: 'She's gunnying in to her hymn-book like if she's going blind.' To *geek* or to *gake* means 'to look fixedly, with specific purpose': 'Close the curtains; we don't want everybody gaking in!' There is a rather similar verb which is not recorded in the language of the Anglo-Saxons, but appears in Dutch as *kijken* 'to look', and in the northern and Scottish dialects as to *keek,* meaning 'to peep'. Travelling from Holland to Harwich on a Dutch ferry, one may be accommodated in an *Uitkijksalon,* which it is tempting to render very closely in the Cornish dialect as 'a room for gaking out of'. A *gake,* like a Scottish *keek,* means 'a peep' or 'a look'. There is also a verb in the Cornish language, *gyky,* but this may itself be a loan from *keek,* and thus a word of non-Celtic origin.

GOODING

I am old enough to have been set handwriting exercises at school. These did not take the form of lines of *pot-crooks* (pothooks) and *hangers* ('S'-shaped loops and links for handwriting practice) such as my grandmother remembered, but of four lines of doggerel verse to be copied:

> Good, better, best,
> Never let it rest,
> Till the good is better,
> And the better, best.

It is interesting that *good, better* and *best* have been made into verbs in the dialect. The first of these is probably now obsolete, though recorded in various glossaries: to go *a-gooding* meant, in less affluent times, to go round just before Christmas begging alms of cooking ingredients or money from richer neighbours. I must confess I have never heard this phrase spoken, but *bettering* and *besting* are certainly heard. To be *bettering* means to be convalescing, or 'on the mend' from an illness, and *besting* means deciding between two alternatives: 'I'm besting, where (whether) to go or no.'

This use of *where* for 'whether' is still very common in the South West. It is a natural elision that has been in the language since Shakespeare's time and before:

> I know not why, except to get the land,
> But once he slandered me with bastardy:
> But *where* I be as true begot or no,
> That still I lay upon my mother's head.

There is a strong tendency to omit, as here, sounds in proximity to the consonant *r*. *Garden* is often pronounced in the South West as *garn, burden* as *burn*. I quote Mrs M. Cuddy, recorder of the St Just-in-Penwith Old Cornwall Society: 'A burn is a large bundle, as much as you can carry on your back.' Again there are plenty of precedents; a stage direction in the Chester Miracle Plays (1400) runs: 'Here Isaack . . . taketh a burne of sticks and beareth after his father.'

GRIZZLE

This is another case, like *chuffed,* of what is ostensibly the same word, having opposite meanings in different dialects.

58

To *grizzle* in Devon and Cornwall does not mean, as it does in some more northern counties, 'to fret, whine or cry'; it means 'to grin' or 'to laugh', especially mockingly. It is characteristic, particularly of mid-Cornwall, to add the particle *up* and to embellish with a simile. People *grizzle up* 'like a a'penny book' or 'like anybody lost a a'penny and found a sixpence'.

This addition of *up*, sometimes adding a note of disparagement, is one of the most characteristic and abiding features of the Cornish dialect. Besides *grizzling up* there is *talking up*, meaning 'talking foolishly' – 'I can't abide anybody talking up so weak' – and *whispering up*, meaning 'whispering inaudibly', to the annoyance of the listener. To *look up wisht* (see *wisht*) is to look eagerly for what one will not get: 'The dear chield was looking up wisht for a sweet like all the others had.'

Finally, there is the expression to *cut up*, meaning 'to talk in a pseudo-refined accent'. There is always somebody in the keenly critical, if ultimately charitable, atmosphere of a village, ready to 'take off' such 'cutting up'.

HEALERS

Reading a Victorian glossary, such as the joint volume published in 1880 for the English Dialect Society by Miss M. Courtney (West Cornwall) and Thomas Q. Couch (East Cornwall), is rather like looking at an old school photograph. Some words, like some children on the photo, we recognise easily, others are less familiar; we cannot, in the dialect phrase, 'call them home'. Our grandparents used these words regularly, but our fathers and mothers do not; or if they do, they add that saddest of qualifiers, 'as the old people used to say'.

My grandparents' generation was more fond than later ones of practical jokes. If someone whisked away another person's property, handing it on to a third person to hide, both would be condemned with the phrase, 'Healers is as bad as stealers' (the two words rhyming with 'jailers'). This vanishing word *heal* is quite distinct from the ordinary standard word meaning 'to cure'. It is an Anglo-Saxon verb meaning 'to hide' or 'to cover up' (the word *hell,* incidentally, is related). It survives today in standard English in the gardener's phrase 'to *heel* plants in', that is, to cover the naked portion of the stem with earth, but the word is now mistakenly associated with the heel of the foot. The Tudor topographer of Cornwall, Carew, used the word *healing* (a modern dialect variant is *helling*), meaning 'roofing, covering'. As he puts it: 'For covering of houses there are three sorts of stone, which from that use take the name of healing stones.'

The root is not vanishing completely without trace for there is a Dutch word *helen* still in regular use, meaning 'to conceal', and they also have a proverb: 'De heler is zo schuldig (guilty) als de steler.'

HER AND US

There is no doubt of the great variation within the dialects of Devon and Cornwall. Even such evidence as remains today suggests that it would be quite wrong to speak of two west-country dialects divided by the River Tamar. A more interesting and profitable set of boundaries has been suggested by Dr Martyn Wakelin, formerly associated with the *SED*. He recommends that we consider the old hundred boundaries, which are to be found on many old maps. Taking these as guides, we can divide Cornwall dialectally into three parts: first, the hundreds of Penwith and Kerrier, west of Truro, where the influence of the old Celtic language on vocabulary and intonation is strongest, but also, paradoxically, where the pronunciation is in many ways closer to standard English because English was acquired there late; secondly, the two mid-Cornwall hundreds of Powder and Pydar, comprising the area east of Truro to a line running roughly from the estuary of the Camel to the estuary of the Fowey; thirdly, the remaining five hundreds of East Cornwall. (If this seems a somewhat indiscriminate lumping together of the hundreds of East Cornwall, we must remember that, as Charles Henderson maintained, the five East Cornwall hundreds were originally only two – Trigg and Wivel.)

An important distinguishing mark of East Cornwall is the pronunciation of the vowel in *do* or *you*, with the characteristically Devonian (and also French) sound, phonetically [y:]. West of the Fowey and Camel estuaries, this vowel is generally like standard English. Not quite so good a guide to the provenance of a dialect speaker, but fairly reliable nevertheless, is the use of *her* for *she* and *us* for *we* before verbs, which again tends to be East Cornwall or Devon usage, but not mid-Cornwall or West Cornwall. For Devon, one can cite that repository of amusing dialect anecdote, Cecil Torr's *Small Talk at Wreyland*:

> Many of the people here had never seen an olive tree before, and were curious about its fruit: so I gave them olives to try. One comment was: 'Well, Mrs——'d never have christened her daughter Olive, if her'd a-tasted one of they.'

For *us* instead of *we*, one can quote the old song 'Tavistock Goosey Fair':

> Us clain'd ourself up vitty,
> Us shav'd and gress'd our hair,
> And off us goes
> In our Sunday clo'es
> To Tavistock Goosey Fair.

It is thus in Devon, rather than Cornwall, that the most complete reversal of the case of pronouns occurs. A devout Devonian explained to Cecil Torr: 'Us didn't love He, 'twas Him loved we.'

In the South West, however, although *us* occurs for *we*, it does not occur for the possessive *our*, which remains as in 'gress'd our hair'. Usage like 'Shall us take us teas?' is Midlands and northern, not westcountry.

JINGLE

'I had to drive seven miles in a thing that only exists South of the Limerick Junction, and is called a *jingle*. A jingle is a square box of painted canvas with no back to it, because, as was humorously explained to me, you must have some way to get into it; and I had to sit sideways in it.'

The author of this particular passage, from one of Somerville and Ross's colourful works on Irish life, was misinformed in thinking that a jingle existed only in Southern Ireland. It is known in Australia and it is certainly known in Cornwall, though the Cornish jingle is not covered or hooded as, according to the *EDD*, it is in Ireland. A pony and jingle used to be a common sight; one stage, in terms of status, above a donkey and wheels.

Alas! the donkey and wheels, like the pony and jingle, is almost never seen today. As early as the 1930s Bernard Walke reports the comment of an old man in Sennen: "'Tis all changed. They old motors have done it. They have spoilt the road for a dunkey.'

JONEYS

It is not only when articles are disused or devalued that a word or phrase is lost. It can happen that when an object increases in general esteem a depreciative word is discarded. Twenty-five years ago it was possible to go round to household sales (often held in dwelling-houses, and much enjoyed by the inquisitive) and there buy such things as china dogs and Staffordshire figures for a few shillings.

The word for all such knick-knacks, but perhaps especially for the Staffordshire figures, is *joneys*, quoted only from Devon in the *EDD*, but known in Cornwall as well. The *EDD* quotation, from Sarah Hewett (1892), exactly shows the status of such articles in those days: 'Loramussy, whatever due 'ee squander yer money 'pon these old joneys vur?' Now that *joneys* sometimes fetch as many pounds as formerly they did pence, the contemptuous word is being dropped.

KIDDLEY-WINK

'Where does this road lead to?' I asked of the man.
'Dun knaw, zur, I'm sure, but they do zay as 'ow it do go to Waadbrudge.'

62

'Wadebridge, eh? Do you know how far it is away?'

'No, zur, I doan't for I never bin mor'n vive mile away from Treloggas, which is my home, zur, but my master es a bit of a traveller, zur. He've bin to Bodmun, and he do zay as 'ow Waadbrudge es fifteen mile on' . . .

'And is there a public-house anywhere near?'

'Iss, zur, 'bout three mile on thurs a kiddley-wink that do belong to Tommy Dain.'

The questioner here is Roger, eponymous hero of *Roger Trewinion* by Joseph Hocking, the Daphne du Maurier or Winston Graham of his generation. His rustic informant seems disorientated beyond the usual wont of rustics, although at least he does not give the standard cagey Cornish reply, 'Well, where've you come from now?', or perhaps the even less helpful 'Well, to tell 'ee the trewth, if I was goin' to Wadebridge, I wouldn't start from here!'

However, it is chiefly the word *kiddley-wink* that is worth considering here. Wright defines it as 'an unlicensed cider or beer-shop; a low public-house or tavern'. The atmosphere of the *kiddley-wink* was furtive, for even if it had a licence it would not be to sell spirits. 'Cap'n' Marshel Arthur, in his authentic story *Piper's Pit*, notes in passing that in the mid-Cornwall area 'the kiddley-wink . . . though only supposed to sell beer, yet served smuggled brandy from Padstow "under the bar"'.

Mr H. L. Douch, in *Old Cornish Inns*, offers two explanations of *kiddley-wink*; I give here the one I consider to be the likelier of these. He quotes from *The Cornishman* (17 Nov 1881): 'At the time the name arose the beershops were not all kept by honest dames, for they were then fond of keeping a little smuggled brandy, which was put in the kettle, so as to deceive the officers of the law; and those who were in the secret, when they came into the room, and wanted some of the brandy, would *wink at the kettle*. Thence arose the term "Kettle and Wink" or "Kiddley-wink".' The word *kiddley* by itself means what is known in the North of England as *pobs* or *pobbies*, that is, bread and milk.

'One and All', it has been pointed out, is as wildly inappropriate a motto as Cornwall could have. Enmity between neighbouring communities has always been part of the air one breathes in Cornwall, and the list of feuds is a long one: Camborne against Redruth, Padstow against Wadebridge, St Austell against St Blazey, and so on. My native village of Roche maintained hostilities with nearby St Dennis which broke out into fighting, at public fêtes and other occasions, when St Dennis people taunted Rochers with being *knuckly-downs*. This somewhat dubious reputation extended over the whole mid-Cornwall area. A. L. Rowse recalls his father as saying 'In Roche they do knuckly down 'pon one knee', and even within the last few years a St Dennis man refused to come to Roche to live, giving as his reason 'I don't want to go up there among they old knuckly-downs.'

As I have it, the tradition relates to an occasion when some Roche yokels attended divine service in St Dennis church and did not kneel at the right place in the ceremony. The parish clerk of St Dennis was reduced to calling out, 'Knuckly down all ye Rochers!' *Knuckly-downs* they have been ever since. But Roche had a rallying cry in opposition; it was *sloany-pie*, sloes being the only kind of fruit which the rather bleak downs around St Dennis will support. It is curious to find Dr Johnson making this same taunt to Boswell about the infertility of Boswell's native Scotland: 'Pray now, are you able to bring the sloe to perfection?'

Local antipathies among the Bodmin Moor villages are enshrined in rhymes:

> Linkinhorne, where the devil was born,
> North Hill, where he lives still.

This foisting of the devil on a village goes back a very long way. In the Cornish play on the life of Meriasek, patron saint of Camborne, *Bewnans Meriasek* (1504), a servant of Meriasek's arch-enemy, the heathen Teudar, announces his intention of sacrificing a tom-cat to Jove:

> Thum du iovyn in y fath
> me a offren lawen cath
>   ny yl boys guel legessa
> me as droys a voruelys
> le may fue an iovle elys.

> To my god, Jove, in his face
> I will offer a tom-cat
> There cannot be a better to catch mice.
> I have brought it from Morval
> A place where the devil has been anointed.

Vorvelys, allowing for the initial mutation of the Celtic languages, is *Morvelys*, ie probably *Morval* in East Cornwall.

Such recognisably local references are rare. The *Ordinalia* are not strongly Cornish in detail or atmosphere. Only occasionally does an odd line remind us that the authors and actors of these plays were westcountrymen. One delightful bit of Cornishry does occur, however, in the second of the three *Ordinalia*, the Passion play, at the point where Caiaphas, the high priest, is conferring about what to do with the thirty pieces of silver that Judas has thrown back at him and which, being blood-money, cannot go into the treasury. Caiaphas's crozier-bearer (the plays, like all medieval religious dramas, are full of anachronisms), who has earlier been described with the words 'connygh yu ow tysputys' (cunning he is in disputing), now speaks up:

> yma *goon* vras thy'mmo vy
> me a's guerth theugh yredy
> a thek-warn-ugans sterlyn

> There is a large *down* of mine
> I will sell it to you now
> for thirty sterling.

This, of course, is the potter's field (Matthew 27: 6–8), but a *goon* is essentially barren land, as in Goonhilly, Goonhavern and Northgoonbarrow. This crozier will do well; he is the prototype of the *jobber* or *dealer* who never lets a chance slip.

More seriously, there is one passage in the Passion play of

the *Ordinalia* which brings home to the Cornish reader the humiliation inflicted at the Crucifixion:

> me a vyn y thyscuthe
> hag yn spyt thotho true
> war y fas ha'y dev lagas.

> I will uncover Him
> and in spite spit at Him
> on His face and His two eyes.

'Right in his face and eyes', as we say.

LAUNDER

Not long ago, an enthusiast from the newly-formed Institute of Cornish Studies came exploring for remains of medieval buildings in the mid-Cornwall area formerly known as Blackmore. It was a forlorn hope, for the moors, already turned upside-down in the search for tin, iron, copper, wolfram and even, more recently, uranium, are now half-covered in china-clay dumps. But there have always been industrial workings here. In the words of Sabine Baring-Gould, 'Hardly a gully has not been *streamed,* every river-bed has been turned over.' Carew described the streaming process in 1602:

> The stream . . . is made to fall by certain degrees . . . upon each of which at every descent lieth a green turf, three or four feet square and one foot thick. On this the tinner layeth a certain portion of the sandy tin and with his shovel softly tosseth the same to and fro, that through this stirring the water which runneth over it may wash away the light earth from the tin, which of a heavier substance lieth fast on the turf . . . After it is thus washed, they put the remnant into a wooden dish, broad, flat and round . . . and having two handles fastened at the sides, by which they softly shog the same to and fro in the water between their legs as they sit over it . . . Some of later time . . . do cause certain boys to stir it up and down with their feet, which worketh the same effect.

The memory of all this vigorous, if rather rheumaticky, activity is preserved in phrases like 'a stream of rain', 'stream-

66

ing a few things through', as the housewife still says when washing clothes, and the common double epithet *streaming-leaking*, meaning 'very wet': 'Why, Miss Ruby, you'm *streamin'-leakin''* one of Q's characters exclaims.

Tin streaming was carried on until comparatively recently on St Agnes beach, and there are still tin-streams in operation in the Camborne–Redruth area. The process of tin-streaming and tin extraction also involved the use of wooden aqueducts known as *launders*, a word that, like many mining terms (*core, bounds, level,* for example), is from French. *Launder* is more likely to be encountered now in the meaning of 'a rainwater gutter' made of iron rather than wood; the *OED* illustrates this usage from a publication entitled *Blizzard of 1891*: 'Icicles hung inches long from windowsills and launders of the houses.'

Another word from mining, that seasonally occurs to me as ripe for extension to standard English, concerns what is laid on ice-bound roads in winter and is variously called sand, grit, gravel or small stones. Such commodities have been the business of Cornwall for centuries, so it is not surprising that Cornishmen describe such things with fair precision, and have useful dialect words such as *skimpings*. 'Skimmings of the light ore in the dressing process' is the technical definition, but the word can be, and often is, applied to the type of small stones which are too big for gravel but too small to be dignified by the title of stones, still less of American *rocks*.

LEWTH

In recent years there has been a tendency in Cornwall to depart from tradition in the matter of locating a dwelling-house. The traditional view has been very well put in dialect by Anne Treneer in *Old Mr Trebilcock,* one of her two dialect stories:

You do drop down by the ash trees in the little *lew* place where Rosemanoweth is. They didn' cock the houses right up in the air in the old days; they knawed better'n that. I wouldn' have a house if you was to give 'un to me if he was cocked up in the air. Tha's neither here nor there of course; but what I mean to say is, Rosemanoweth was in the *lewth*.

Lewth, is from *lew* as *dryth* is from *dry*. The OE *(ge)hleow* meant 'warm, sunny', and the present meaning of 'sheltered' developed from this, perhaps by association, in some instances, with the more nautical *lee*. The English names of many west-country settlements bear out this predilection for warmth and shelter. Pleasant Streams, Riverside, Happy Valley, Sunny Corner; such names are often at least two hundred years older than Moor View, Sea View etc.

The word *lew,* for me, has two main associations. The first of these is this poem in south-western dialect by Eden Phillpotts, which deserves to be better known:

Man's Days

A sudden wakin', a sudden weepin',
A li'l suckin', a li'l sleepin';
A cheel's full joys an' a cheel's short sorrows,
Wi' a power o' faith in gert tomorrows.

Young blood red-hot an' the love of a maid,
One glorious day as'll never fade;
Some shadows, some sunshine, some triumph, some tears,
And a fatherin' weight o' the flyin' years.

Then old man's talk o' the days behind 'ee,
Your darter's youngest darter to mind 'ee;
A li'l dreamin', a li'l dyin'
A li'l lew corner o' airth to lie in.

The other, and less sobering, association is with carol-singing. The technique in carol-singing, as Thomas Hardy knew, is to 'go quietly, so as to strick up all of a sudden, like spirits'. So, quietly, down the path of a hopefully generous householder we would go, on a cold Christmas Eve. 'Come in here boys,' the leader would whisper, 'come in the lewth; 'tis lew's a box in here. Now, hold hard! Ready?' Then would follow one of those carols with both words and music in what might be called provincial Baroque, sung to an involved tune, probably by Thomas Merritt of Illogan.

See in the East a star appears
Which breaks the gloom of num'rous years,
Bids the deep shades of darkness fly
And speaks the Prince of Glory nigh.

How well Thomas Hardy understood all this! 'Forty breaths, and then "O what unbounded goodness!" number fifty-nine,' says the chief carol-singer, William Dewey, in *Under the Greenwood Tree*.

Complicated tunes with interlacing counterpoint have always been popular in Cornwall. Merritt's carols tend to be in the sub-Handelian tradition which John Wesley had earlier deplored. In 1765 Wesley complained that 'all over Cornwall' the Methodists were singing the words of 'Praise the Lord ye blessed ones', to a tune 'so full of repetition and flourishes that it can scarce be sung with devotion'. One of the difficulties was that such tunes necessitated distortion of the words. As a correspondent in the *Bible Christian Magazine* pointed out in 1877: 'Often very laughable effects are obtained in this way. Fancy a congregation having to sing the line "And take the pilgrim home", as "And take the pil——, and take the pil——".' Modern developments, in language as in life, have done nothing to weaken the force of this objection.

LIDDEN

It is always dangerous to assume that a word is obsolete; but one which was occasionally heard thirty years ago, and probably never heard today, is *lidden* or *ledden*. It is defined in Jago's *The Ancient Language and the Dialect of Cornwall* as 'an oft told tale' or something 'harped on one string', as in 'that old lidden again'. As I have heard the word, however, the meaning was 'incomprehensible rigmarole' – 'he talked up a lot of old ledden'. The word was borrowed from *Latinum* (Latin) very early in the history of the English language, being common in Old and Middle English. Clearly there is great continuity here. *Ledden* both connotes and embodies, in its etymology and development, a peasant incomprehension of the mysteries of the medieval church service. The pejorative implications appear early; in *Piers Plowman,* for example:

Though he crye to Cryst . . . I leue
His ledne be in owre lordes ere lyke a pyes chiterynge.

This last word, incidentally, a variant of *chattering,* will be very familiar in the westcountry, whether predicated of the jabbering of birds, as here, or of the scolding of humans. Sarah Hewett quotes: 'They chillern chitter like a tree vull of sparrows.' One can also, for some reason, 'chitter like a pickpocket'.

Most westcountry readers would have some idea also of what the author of *Piers Plowman* meant by *chibolles* in 'benes and baken apples, chibolles and cheruelles'. They would be familiar with *chibol onions,* those spring onions which, eaten in the early stages of their growth, are doubtless very like the chibol proper which Langland knew. Dialect usage can also explain what at first sight might seem vain repetition in the following *Piers Plowman* lines, where 'Long Will' is asked what farm work he is capable of:

Canstow . . .
Mowe other *mowen* other make bond to sheves?

The first verb, *mowe,* is 'to cut grass or corn'; the second, *mowen,* means 'to put in mows or stacks'. For those of us who have helped, in a *catchy* season, to build up head high those temporary ricks afield known as handmows, the word will have a special significance, reminding us of a continuity of experience with our earlier literature, so recently broken. In West Cornwall, according to the *SED,* a *mow* is a small corn-stack made in the field, smaller than the more permanent *rick.* In parts of mid-Cornwall, however, to quote the survey, ''tis a mow of corn and a rick of hay'.

In the book which conveys the atmosphere of life in mid-Cornwall 100 years ago better than any other I know, *The Life and Reminiscences of C. T. T., Luxulyan, Cornwall,* the author describes the uniform of the private school he attended at St Austell, which included a silk hat. When he wore his hat at home in Luxulyan, one old villager exclaimed, 'Here comes Charley Trevail, like a mouse under a *barley-mow.*' Such a hat would be called locally a Par Stack, from the tallest and blackest chimney-stack in the china-clay area, at Par. 'Cap'n' Marshel Arthur, writing in the magazine *Old Cornwall*, recalls that the first prize for *wrasslin* at St Stephen's Feast used to be a Par Stack.

LOGGAN-STONE

There seems to be no general agreement as to what the verb to *log* means in the South West. In the past it has certainly meant 'to rock to and fro' – in Devon one could speak of 'logging a cradle' – and it was in general use in Cornwall in the last century for the roll of a drunken man. These meanings are enough to account for the *loggan-stone*, the kind of stone which William Mason wrote of in his dramatic poem 'Caractacus':

                          Thither, youths,
    Turn your astonish'd eyes; behold yon huge
    And unhewn sphere of living adamant,
    Which, poised by magic, rests its central weight
    On yonder pointed rock: firm as it seems,
    Such is the strange and virtuous property,
    It moves obsequious to the gentlest touch
    Of him whose breath is pure; but to a traitor,
    Though even a giant's prowess nerved his arm,
    It stands as fixed as Snowdon.

It was the nephew of another eighteenth-century poet, a Lieutenant Goldsmith RN, who scandalised the Duchy in 1824 by dislodging its most famous loggan-stone, the one in St Levan parish, to disprove Borlase's statement that 'it is morally impossible that any lever, or indeed force, however applied in a mechanical way, can remove it from its present position'. The Admiralty arranged for the stone to be replaced and sent Goldsmith the bill, which he was paying for the rest of his life. There is a loggan-stone on Rowtor, and there is said to be another on Helman Tor.

Logging, however, seems to have developed another dialect

71

meaning. I know it in the sense of 'hauling' or 'carrying with difficulty': 'You'm never going to log that lot up the hill!' This may, of course, be a confusion with *lug*, as in Hamlet's 'I'll lug the guts into the neighbour room.'

There is no doubt that *loggan* is, at root, not Celtic in origin but an English dialect verb, although W. B. Lockwood sees the influence of late Cornish in the development from *logging* to *loggan*. There was a clear tendency, in the last stages of the language, for the indistinct 'e' of the final, unstressed syllable to become 'a'. Thus Middle Cornish *steren*, 'a star', becomes Late Cornish *steran*; also in the West Cornwall dialect writing, *kindness* can appear as *kindnass*.

LOUSTER

Phrases such as 'They that can't schemy must louster', or 'I can louster and fouster but I can't tiddly', are very common usage in the Cornish dialect. Both *louster* and *fouster* (*whispering* and *tispering* are a comparable rhymed combination) mean 'to work hard', though *louster* is more common. The *EDD* quotes appositely from *The Cornishman* of 4 March 1893: 'Defendant asked for time to pay, as he only earns 3s. a week and his father is a lousterer on the town' (ie one who does manual work with wages chargeable to the parish, or perhaps the inmate of a workhouse). To *tiddly* means to do the lighter kinds of housework.

The extra suffix on verbs like *schemy* and *tiddly* is a common feature of the dialects of the South West. F. T. Elworthy noted, in his two-volume publication for the English Dialect Society *The Dialect of West Somerset,* that this extra syllable is added to verbs which have no object. I remember an old lady saying, 'I must sit down by the fire and griddly a bit' ie 'get warm'. There were originally two OE endings for an infinitive: *-an* or *-ian* (ME *-en* and *-ien*). Thus the ancestor of *to sing* was *singan*, but that of *to till* was *tilian*. Even so, this historical aspect has been obscured by what became in effect a westcountry dialect rule, that verbs with no object, whatever their ancestry, could have the extra syllable, whereas verbs with an object could not. Thus *till*, which always takes an object, never has the extra 'y', though historically (OE *tilian*) we might expect it; but the 'y' is added, quite un-historically, to intransitive verbs: 'I bain't one to *gardeny*; but I do generally *teal* the garden every spring.'

There is an additional reason for this extra syllable in the Cornish dialect: it occurs with both transitive and intransitive verbs loaned into the Cornish language. In the Passion play of the *Ordinalia* the sign 'Jesus of Nazareth, King of the Jews' is put up over the head of Christ at the crucifixion with the words:

> drou e thy'mmo the *tackye*
> a vgh y pen gans mur greys
> may hallo pup y *redye*
> gour ha benen kekyffrys.

> Bring it to me *to fasten*
> Above His head with much strength
> That all may *read it*
> Man and woman likewise.

There is a curious word which one can associate with *louster*; this is *labbut*, of uncertain provenance and found, it seems, only in Cornwall. It means a drudge, a menial of the lowest grade; someone who, in the vulgar dialect phrase, is 'tied to the bull's arse and shit to death'. The word is not rare. One still hears expressions like: 'They got he there for a labbut, that's all, to help with the rough work.'

LUE!

Now that battery hen farming is so widespread, that most characteristic country sound, the early morning crowing of the cock ('the kok, that orloge is of thorpes lyte', as Chaucer puts it), is rarer. In rural mid-Cornwall, however, one can still be awakened by cries of 'Hoke! Hoke! Hoke!' This is a very localised way of calling cattle; farther west, the cry is 'Coop!' or 'Cope!' and farther east, it is 'Hoit!' These cries are all recorded in the *SED*, as are those for calling pigs (Choog! Choog!) and hens (Tiki! Tiki!), which have given westcountry children the affectionate terms *choogy-pig* and *ticky-fowl*. Anne Treneer records this rendering by a local preacher of the story of the Gadarene swine: 'And then all they pigs they took to their heels, screeching, and went slap bang over cliff. And 'twadn' no good then for 'em to cry "Chug, chug!" and rattle the handle of the bucket. They pigs never come home no more!'

There is one call, however, which the *SED* does not include but which is recorded by Mr Tom Tremewan in his reminiscences of old Perranporth, *Cornish Youth: Memories of a Perran Boy*, published in 1968. He describes the scene when corn is being harvested; as the square of uncut grain dwindles, the rabbits imprisoned amid the stalks make a bolt for the hedge, across the unfamiliar *arrish* (stubble). Men, boys and dogs all rush towards them shouting and barking, and the poor creatures, paralysed with fear, 'go to lie' or 'quatty down', remaining rigid in the stubble until picked up and despatched with one smart blow on the back of the neck.

The cry of the pursuers here was 'Lue! lue! lue!', a call which is not peculiar to Cornwall. Henry Williamson in his *Tales from a Devon Village* records it being used at a badger hunt, and the cry is also found, rendered in print as *loo*, in Suffolk. It may well be an abbreviated form of 'view halloo', as in the song 'D'ye ken John Peel'.

MAIDENS

Northern words like *lad* and *lass* only occur in the west-country as importations. R. S. Hawker's 'Song of the Western Men' is rousing stuff, and the nearest thing to a national anthem we have, but the last line of the first verse strikes a jarring note:

> A good sword and a trusty hand,
> A merry heart and true!
> King James's men shall understand
> What Cornish *lads* can do.

The real Cornish equivalent of *lads* is *boys*. 'There are no

74

men in Cornwall,' it has been said, 'they are all boys.' There is also an old rhyme:

> Good luck to all the Cornish boys
> That never yet was beaten.
> A pasty may they never want,
> Nor stomachs for to ait'n.

It is not uncommon for even elderly husbands and wives to address each other affectionately as *boy* and *maid*, much as in Yorkshire they might say *lad* and *lass*. Even the plant southernwood, traditionally known elsewhere as *lad's love*, is known in Somerset, Devon, Cornwall and Hardy's Dorset (see his short story 'The Fiddler of the Reels') as *boy's love*. As Edward Thomas knew (see his poem *Old Man*) southernwood has a powerfully evocative, bitter-sweet smell. Elworthy in his *The Dialect of West Somerset* conjures up most pungently a vanished world with his entry under *boy's love*: 'A very great favourite with the village belles. In the summer, nearly all carry a spray of it half wrapped in a white handkerchief, in their hand to church. In fact, a village church on a hot Sunday afternoon quite reeks with it.' In standard English, *maid*, occurring as it does only in phrases like 'old maid' or with the meaning of 'a servant', has lost much of the warmth which it still retains dialectally (and archaically). A vestige of this warmth remains when, in Henry James's *The Portrait of a Lady*, the English aristocrat, Lord Warburton, introduced to Osmond's daughter, exclaims: 'What a dear little maid!' Wright notes in the *EDD* that in Somerset an old woman might say, speaking of a married daughter, 'I have not seen my maid this while.'

As a variant of *maids*, the word *maidens* (often pronounced 'med'ns') tends to occur in the plural, often with a more collective force. 'Coosing the med'ns' was a traditional Sunday evening pastime, certain places being especially frequented for this purpose. At St Dennis in mid-Cornwall, for example, there was what was cynically known as the Market. The late 'Cap'n' Marshel Arthur explains the origin of the name: 'Piper, who was not "chapel-going", would be strolling along between Nanpean river-walk and Lestowrack Downs, where the young people from the Higher Quarter walked to meet the young people of St. Dennis after service on fine summer and autumn evenings. This stretch of road was called (and is still) by the cynical older folk the Cattle-Market, because young people met there and paired off, sometimes ending in the marriage-market.'

It is all vanished now as though it had never been. For who would go a-courting today without the aid of the internal-combustion engine? To quote T. S. Eliot:

> Every son would have his motor-cycle
> And daughters ride away on casual pillions.

MAIL

Westcountry memories are long. People who behave out-landishly are 'fit to frighten the French', as they doubtless were in Napoleon's day, and from the same era comes the local equivalent of 'never' – 'when Nelson get his eye back'. Those who move quickly 'go like the Mail', ie the mail coach, a comparison which is heard more widely, as in the Welsh *mynd fel y Mel*. Someone who has cooked a large dinner is told: 'You got enough here for Kitchener's army.' Many men were christened Kitchener in honour of this national hero, or Redvers, after a more local one of the same Boer war period, General Redvers Buller of Crediton. By far the commonest of these Christian names from surnames was Wesley, but even this is now rare and the other two have died out almost completely.

MAZED

Mazed is the only Cornish dialect word that I have discovered in John Wesley's *Journal*. An entry for September 1755 reads:

I called on W. Rowe in Breage . . . 'Twelve years ago,' he said, 'I was going over Gulval Downs, and I saw many people together, and I asked what was the matter, and they told me a man was going to preach. And I said, 'To be sure it is some mazed man.' But when I saw you I said, 'Nay, this is no mazed man.'

Maze(d), of course, means 'mad'; and there are two comparisons, 'so maze as a sheep' and 'so maze as a curly' (curlew), differentiating the stupid and the raving kinds of madness. This letter written by Gilbert White suggests why a curlew is used in the comparison: 'Any evening you may see them (curlews) around the village, for they make a clamour which may be heard a mile.' My parents' generation used *mazegerry*, both as a noun and adjective: 'He's a proper mazegerry', or ''tis a mazegerry business'. The second element is comparable with Middle English words like *child-gered.* King Arthur, at the beginning of the medieval romance *Sir Gawain and the Green Knight,* is said to be 'somquat child-gered', ie 'having rather childish manners, somewhat childish or skittish'.

For loss of wits in senility there is a special dialect adjective, *totelish*: 'He's getting old and totelish.'

MAZZARD

A name now almost lost, which formerly gave extra precision to south-western dialect, is *mazzard,* for the black cherry, generally sweeter than the red. Wright notes, in the *EDD*: 'In some places there are fairs called after the fruit because it is in season when they take place.' Such a mazzard fair was Roche July Fair, when people bought black cherries, just as they bought onions at the October Onion Fair. The three fairs (there was another in May) continued until quite recently.

It was possible to look over the wall of the village school into the Fair Park, as it was called, on the manor farm of Tregarrick (*carek* is Cornish for 'rock'). There we could see the auctioneers and cattle-dealers, and the gipsies and horse-traders running the animals up and down to show their paces. Until the early years of this century *gossies* – a now meaningless word formerly used for small ponies ten to twelve hands high, which roamed wild and bred on the Goss and Tregoss

Moors – were rounded up and sold at the October Fair. Here too was the parish pound, for such animals as went astray. The person impounding cattle fixed a charge to cover the damage done to his property; if this should be disputed, the damage was computed by a valuer agreed to by both parties. The amount had to be paid before the impounded animals were given up by the pound-keeper, the tenant of Tregarrick farm. The owner of the cattle had to pay the keeper for all food and attention given whilst the beast remained impounded.

The word *park*, ultimately from Old French, was taken into Cornish as a regular word for a field and still survives in field names with a descriptive adjective afterwards on the Celtic pattern. *Park Woon*, for example, is 'moor field', with *woon* a mutated form of *goon*, 'a moor'. Today there is a curious reluctance, which may be linguistic memory, to use the word *park* of the more urbanised modern pleasure grounds. Recreation ground or playing field are often preferred synonyms.

There may be a similar memory of Celtic Cornish in the preference which the *SED* notes for *cows-house* (Cornish *bowjy*) against Devon *shippen* (OE *scypen*). Other words formed on this *-house* pattern are quite common: one small-holding I know has a cows-house, a sticks-house, a lathe-house, a trap-house and a coal-house. The word *bowjy* or *bougie*, for a rough shelter or barn for sheep and cattle, often in a field, was recorded in the *EDD* but not by the *SED*, and may no longer be understood. This word *bowjy* is etymologically the exact Cornish equivalent of English *cow-house*. By Celtic initial mutation, the *jy* here is the same as *chy* meaning 'house', recalling those many post-Gorsedd names, *Chy an Garek, Chy an Mengleth, Chy an Mor* ('house by the rock, the stone quarry, the sea'), which it is now fashionable to have as house-names.

MEAT

The word *meat* occurs in dialect in its older English sense (rather like the biblical *sweetmeats*) of food generally, not merely the flesh of animals. It can also be used as a verb; a regular chore on farms is to *meat* (pronounce as *mate*) the pigs and fowls. Idlers are told: 'Do something for your meat, if you get your drink for nothing', while thrifty people save up odds and ends on the grounds that they may come in handy, and that in any case 'they won't eat no meat'. Broad beans are known in East Cornwall as *meat beans*, sometimes still to be heard with the pronunciation of *mate banes*.

Rabbits' meat (sometimes used contemptuously of salads) is any green herb used to feed tame rabbits, especially dandelion plants, whose milky roots are known as *milky dashels*, to be distinguished from *dashels* proper, which are thistles.

MENHIR

The word *menhir* means in Cornish 'long stone', the kind of long and upright monumental stone that was more numerous formerly. Originally they must have had a religious purpose; later they marked parish boundaries and later still, they were removed to make granite gate-posts. Sometimes the word is used in its English form as *longstone*, as in Great Longstone China-Clay Works, but it is *menhir* that has given two surnames, both common in mid-Cornwall, Mennear and Manhire. My grandfather, who had an antiquarian's instinct for such matters, always said that the former was the original surname, but that when the Mennears got on in the world they moved down from the Higher Quarter to the villages and took on the name Manhire, with its English implication of 'employer'. To this day, you are more likely to find, in mid-Cornwall, Manhires below the tree-line and Mennears above it. The fact that Manhire was never an English name is shown by the accent. It is only non-natives who accent Manhire like Mansfield; both Mennear and Manhire are pronounced in the true Cornish way, with the accent on the second syllable.

This use of *long* in the vertical sense was common in earlier English, and has given us the English surname Long and Scottish Laing for ancestrally tall men. The Cornish equivalent, in the predicative position, was *en hyr*, which yields the fairly common surname Annear.

79

Shakespeare used the word *mich* meaning 'to play truant'. 'Shall the blessed sun of heaven prove a micher and eat blackberries?' asks Falstaff in *Henry IV* part I. The picking of berries was clearly a traditional pastime, and perhaps a motive, for the truant. The *EDD* records from North Molton in North Devon the rhyme:

> Blackberry michard,
> Blueberry snail,
> All the dogs in the town
> Hang to thy tail.

In Cornwall the variant *minch* or *minchy* is more common than *mich*. I think that Q could not resist departing from normal mid-Cornwall usage to assert continuity from Elizabethan English in a passage like the following from *Troy Town*:

> You mou't clane their faces an' grease their hair as you wou'd
> . . . but turn your back, an' they'd be mitchin' in a brace of
> shakes an' 'way to go for Coombe beach.

The expression '*'way to go*', an infinitive instead of a full verb, is still often heard. There are precedents for it both in earlier English and in the Celtic languages. Here is Chaucer telling the tragic story of Antony and Cleopatra in *The Legend of Good Women*:

> Antony is schent, and put him to the flyghte
> And al his folk to go, that best go mighte.

It is usually the verb *to go* which is abbreviated in this way, and it is with this verb, too, that we find another curious survival, although it has been very imperfectly recorded. This is the last vestige of what in Old and early Middle English was the almost universal final consonant of the infinitive, viz, 'n', as in Middle English *gon,* 'to walk, to go'. This consonant is now entirely lost to standard English but survives in the South West with the verb *to go,* nowadays mostly when a vowel follows: 'I must *gone* on', or 'Well, I'll *gone* on up to bed.' This earlier English usage is echoed in the Chester play *The Deluge,* in which Noah says:

> This window I will shut anon,
> And into my chamber will I gone.

MURYANS

Some of the most interesting words in the *SED* are those which are most at risk, appearing only once or twice in the field-workers' records. 'What do you call the amount of hay you cut off at a time for your own use?' they asked. 'A cake of hay', 'a cut of hay' and 'a truss of hay' were common answers, but only in two places, at Egloshayle in Cornwall and Cornwood in West Devon, did they encounter the old word *yafful* (though as a matter of fact, it does still survive also in the far west in the form *jafful*). A *yafful* seems to mean a bundle or armful and probably goes back further than words like *cut* and *cake,* which imply the use of a hay-knife. 'A bundle of straw, a faggot of sticks, a yafful of hay' is correct usage, so an informant in mid-Cornwall tells me; but who will remember these distinctions in a generation?

Another word of increasing rarity is *muryans.* It is only in the hundred of Penwith, in the far west of Cornwall, that the *SED* fieldworkers met this Celtic Cornish word for 'ants'. It is a double plural, for *muryon* – like *mebyon* in *Mebyon Kernow,* 'sons of Cornwall' – is plural already. In the *EDD* there is an amusing story of a West Cornwall Sunday School teacher who was surprised when one of his pupils reacted to the biblical phrase 'There shall be a grievous murrain [ie cattle-plague] in the land', with the words, 'Ants is awful things, ain't 'em?'

Elsewhere in the South West ants are generally called *emmets*; one of those words, like *want* for 'mole', that is so widespread as to be barely dialectal. *Emmets* are the standard comparison for crowds: 'The people is on the beaches on fine week-ends in summer like emmets.'

Talking of doubtful biblical commentaries from West Cornwall reminds one of Billy Bray's alleged interpretation of the text 'In my Father's house are many mansions' (John 14 : 2). 'There you are,' Billy is said to have commented, 'none of your barley bread, brethren – real *manshuns*!' A *manshun,* in West Cornwall, is a batch loaf; a loaf of white bread, not baked in a tin but shaped like a large bun. A variant, common in late Middle English for fine wheat bread, was *manchet.*

MY LOVER

In the first of the three Cornish *Ordinalia,* which deals chiefly with Old Testament subjects, Noah's dove is sent out from the ark. 'Colom whek, glas hy lagas' is the Cornish phrase to describe the dove, using a characteristically Celtic idiom of which, sadly, there is no trace in modern dialect: 'Sweet dove, blue her eyes.' In the 1973 Northcott Theatre production of this play Mrs Noah provided some additional dialogue from the south-western dialect. She produced the bird with the words, 'Come on, *my lover*!' This is the westcountry equivalent of Midlands 'me duck' and Edinburgh 'hen'; neither phrase, clearly, being appropriate in the circumstances! Yet I fear that once again the western expression is dying out first. Westcountry people do not call any of their near and dear 'my lover' these days; one reason may be that the phrase now suggests a paramour. Its use to refer to a dear friend was formerly standard English. Shakespeare's Brutus protests that he loved his friend Julius Caesar even though he killed him: 'As I slew my best lover for the good of Rome, I have the same dagger for myself, when it shall please my country to need my death.'

NEW FANG

I write this phrase with some hesitation, aware that those who recognise it will probably know it as *new vang* (see also *sam-soodled*), though west of Truro the unvoiced consonant 'f' is probably heard. The spelling with 'f' indicates the connection with one of the commonest OE verbs, now largely obsolete, *fon, feng, fangen,* corresponding to our *take, took, taken.*

The older verb has not disappeared without trace. It survives in the noun *fangs,* for instance, by which an animal 'takes' its prey, and also in the adjective *new-fangled,* of which the noun *new fang* is a dialectal variant. This phrase is used contemptuously for something new which 'takes' in the sense that Jane Austen sometimes used the word *take,* that is, 'takes the fancy, becomes a fashion': 'They'll soon get tired of it; 'tis only a new vang.'

The Victorian glossaries nearly all include *fangings* for 'earnings, wages', but this I have never heard.

"OBBY-'OSS'

One of the few places where the extremes of suburban refinement and authentic folk-custom meet nowadays is at the Sidmouth International Folk Dance Festival, held annually at the beginning of August. There colleens dancing Irish jigs rub shoulders with West Indian beaters of oil-drums and state-subsidised Slav dancers. There too is old England; Morris men with bells on their fingers and flowers in their straw hats, twiddling their handkerchiefs. It is very worthy, and also entertaining, but it reminds one a little in its eclecticism of Aldous Huxley's parody of a pop-song:

> What's he to Hecuba?
> Nothing at all.
> That's why there'll be no wedding on Wednesday week
> Way down in old Bengal.

On the last night of the week-long festival, there is a parade of participants along the sea-front. Suddenly, a primitive, atavistic roar is heard at the far end of the town. It is what is described in the *Bewnans Meriasek* of 1504 as *hebyhors hay cowetha* – 'the hobby-horse and his companions' – bus-loads of camp-followers who have driven the 100 miles or so from Padstow across Cornwall and Devon to display their local deity. Their cry is "Oss! 'oss! we 'oss!'

The Padstow horse is of the kind described briefly by Sir Walter Scott in *The Abbot*: 'One fellow, with a horse's head

painted on him, and a tail behind, and the whole covered
with a long footcloth which was supposed to hide the body of
the animal, ambled, carolled, pranced, and played, as he
performed the celebrated part of the Hobby Horse.' The
habit which the horse traditionally has of bumping against
women, or taking them under the cloth-covered rim of the
'body', suggests to the folklorist a parallel with the race that
Mark Antony takes part in at the feast of the Lupercal in
Shakespeare's *Julius Caesar*:

> Forget not in your speed, Antonius,
> To touch Calpurnia; for our elders say,
> The barren, touched in this holy chase,
> Shake off their sterile curse.

In the light of the pitch flares on Sidmouth promenade,
the hobby-horse, who echoes the rhythm of the seasons in
periodically feigning death and then springing to life again,
leaps up for the last time. With a roar, he rushes with his
cowetha over the pebbly beach to the sea as the flaming
torches are 'quenched' in the salt waters.

But May Day of course is, for Padstow and all Padstonians,
the time to see the custom in its true setting. Sir John
Betjeman writes: 'On the day before May Day, green boughs
are put up against the houses. And that night every man and
woman in Padstow is awake with excitement. I knew somebody who was next to a Padstow man in the trenches in the
1914 war. On the night before May Day, the Padstow man
became so excited he couldn't keep still. The old 'obby 'oss
was mounting in his blood and his mates had to hold him
back from jumping over the top and dancing about in No-
man's land.'

When I went as a student to Liverpool, just after World
War II, I lived in 'digs' in primmest Aigburth with a Padstow
man. Normally the most sensible of fellows, at midnight on
30 April he would rouse the landlady and the household with
a rendering of the May Song:

> Rise up, Mrs Bate, I know you well-a-fine,
> For summer is a-come unto day.

You have a shilling in your purse, I wish it were in mine,
In the merry morning of May.

He would go down to town next day with a large tulip in
his button-hole, provoking, as he intended, questions which
he was delighted to answer at length:

'*What* hobby-horse?'
'Padsta 'obby-'oss.'
'Padsta? Never heard of it.'
'Never heard of Padsta? You haven't lived . . .'

In one sense, perhaps, he was right; there is an elemental
life in the hobby-horse which never reaches big cities. But
in Padstow, at least, the hobby-horse is not forgot.

OWN

'I've no patience with people like that. One day all over 'ee,
the next they don't own 'ee.' Such criticisms are often heard
in the South West, where a strong point of recommendation
is to be 'always the same'. To be 'all over a person', of course,
means to be fulsomely affable; more interesting is this dialect
use of to *own* (pronounced, in broad dialect, like the first
syllable of *awning*) in the sense of 'to acknowledge a greeting,
recognise as an acquaintance'. This was once standard English
usage, in centuries when to be cut socially could have more
drastic consequences. Here is Pepys, writing in 1662:

April 27th: Sir W. Pen got trimmed before me, and so took
the coach to Portsmouth, to wait on my Lord Steward to
church. And sent the coach for me back again: so I rode to
church and met my Lord Chamberlaine upon the walls of
the Garrison, who owned and spoke to me.

PADGY-POW

The far west of Cornwall is the area where the original
Cornish language was slowest to die out. Here, as we might
expect, there are more words of Celtic derivation remaining
in the dialect. One such word is *padgy-pow* meaning 'a newt',

known farther east as a *four-legged emmet,* which itself contains the same idea translated into English, for *peswar* and *paw* are the Cornish words for 'four' and 'foot' respectively.

Whidden or *piggy-whidden* is found in the hundreds of Penwith and Kerrier as a term for the runt, or the weakest pig of a litter of farrows; *whidden* descending from Cornish *gwyn* – late Cornish *gwidden* – meaning 'white'. Farther east the runt is known by a variety of names of English derivation: *nestle-bird, nestle-draff, nestle-dris* and *nestle-tripe*

In his book on English dialects Dr Wakelin lists a score of words from Celtic Cornish, along with various other words and expressions, such as the still very common *flam-new* for 'brand new' (Welsh *newydd flam,* Breton *nevez flamm*), which come ultimately from French and Latin, but probably via the Celtic languages. His list, as he would be the first to admit, is not complete, since it consists only of those words recorded by the Leeds Survey. On the other hand, Wright's insertion in the *EDD* of well over 100 words allegedly derived from the Cornish language, certainly includes many that have hardly been heard this century and some very suspicious items indeed.

Dr Wakelin does not include one or two words found throughout the county, such as *clicky* (qv), or *whilky,* for a frog – especially common in the phrase 'blawed up like a whilky' of a conceited person. Behind *whilky* and its variant *quilkin,* recorded by Mrs Kathleen Hawke and others in the phrase 'cold as a quilkin', is Cornish *quylkyn,* 'a frog'. From an elderly West Cornwall couple I learnt, when a boy, another word derived from Celtic Cornish; *biscan,* 'a finger-stall, a sheath for a sore finger' (often made by cutting up an old glove), elsewhere in the West sometimes known as a *hood* or a *huddick.* The two Cornish words here are *bys,* 'finger' and (probably) *gon,* 'sheath'. Dr Wakelin mentions one West Cornwall word that is also common farther east. This is *bannel,* meaning 'broom' (the plant) from Cornish *banal.*

An expression now confined to the two villages of Newlyn and Mousehole (home of Dolly Pentreath) is 'roaring like gelvern', of a fire blazing up a chimney. Nance believed the word to be derived from Cornish *gelforn,* a contraction of *govelforn* 'a smithy furnace'. (The Cornish equivalent of the commonest English surname, Smith, is Angove.)

The Cornish word for 'eye' was *lagas,* and while it does not survive as such, fishermen in Mounts Bay in the far west still apparently speak of a *lagas* with the special meaning of an 'eye' or small patch of blue in an otherwise cloudy and threatening sky. Nance was able to quote the weather-rhyme:

> When a lagas shows in the sky
> 'Tis fining up for dry.

With this we can compare the Welsh phrase *llygedyn olau,* 'a ray of light' (literally 'a little eye of light').

When we come to phrases and idioms rather than individual words, which may go back to the Cornish language, we are on shakier ground. A dialect phrase that mystifies strangers is the still very frequent expression of endearment (commonly used of a small child) 'the dear of him' or 'the dear of her'. One could suggest parallels in Welsh where expressions of commiseration incorporating Welsh *truan* 'a wretch, an unfortunate' occur thus: *Druan ag e(f), druan ohono (fe)* ie 'poor fellow', literally 'wretch of him', and *druan a hi, druan ohono (hi)* 'poor woman', literally 'wretch of her'. From Breton also there are comparable phrases.

In the Celtic languages, unlike English, the normal position of the adjective is after the noun. When, therefore, we encounter the West Cornwall dialect variant *headlight* for 'light-headed, dizzy', we are tempted to compare Welsh *penysgafn,* with the same meaning. In each case the adjective (*light, ysgafn*) follows the noun. It is true that a parallel word-order can occur in English in a limited number of compounds, *headstrong* and *footloose,* for example, but the occurrence of *headlight* in West Cornwall suggests a Celtic pedigree. The Cornish word for 'bare-headed', recorded in the *Bewnans Meriasek,* is *pennoth,* literally 'head bare'.

The Celtic word for 'head', *pen,* may possibly be at the root of another enigmatic dialect phrase, *penny-liggan.* 'He's coming home with *Penny Liggan*', writes Robert Hunt, and he adds in explanation, 'the term was probably *penny-lacking* originally'. I have heard both *penny-lacking* and *penny-leaking* as attempts to rationalise this phrase, but it often occurs in contexts which have nothing to do with money, in the more general sense of 'frustrated, unsuccessful', and Nance may well have been right to look for a Celtic ancestry in *pen helygen*. *Helygen* (the word occurs on its own as a place-name) means 'willow', traditional tree of mourning and regret; so to return *penny-liggan* may mean *pen heligen,* 'with head of willow'. This recalls Desdemona's willow song in *Othello* and an English folk-song in which the swain declares 'All round my hat I shall wear the green willow . . . I shall wear it for my true love who is far, far away.'

PASTY

The *OED* gives two pronunciations; one rhyming with *vasty* and the other with *hasty*. Neither of these pronunciations, however, will do for the Duchy, where they have their own ideas on the subject. Speaking generally, and very untechnically, the nearer you approximate the vowel to an abbreviated sheep's bleat, the more authentic it will sound.

The pasty is a national emblem; far more so than the Cornish choughs which are so prominent in the Gorsedd ceremony. It is the product of a poor, hand-to-mouth, make-do economy. Hence a mixture of amusement and amazement at a certain immigrant (the word *import* is now preferred to *foreigner*, as being more, shall we say, impersonal), who, in a strenuous effort to 'go native', asked, 'What wine should I serve with pasty?' One of those respectable bodies who come to the rescue in embarrassing moments is said to have offered the suggestion, 'A good cup tay is so well's anything, my dear.'

The characteristic oval shape with tapered ends has led to some extension of meaning. A pasty of orange for an orange segment and pasty nuts for Brazil nuts, both seem inevitable to the Cornishman. Traditionally the penalty for children who wet the bed is a mousey-pasty. As the old rhyme has it:

Matthew, Mark, Luke and John
Ate a pasty ten foot long.
Bite 'n once, bite 'n twice,
Oh my gor! 'e's full of mice!

The pasty is versatile and can accommodate any odd scraps. All the guide-books advance the theory (though I have never heard it mentioned except in guide-books) that the Devil does not come into Cornwall for fear of being put in a pasty. The variety of ingredients includes *apple'n spice, apple'n 'inge* (the 'pluck' or 'innards' of a pig), *egg 'n ham* and *licks* (leeks). There is also a *grass pasty,* which tastes better than it sounds, with various herbs, egg and the remains of the last pig-killing.

My favourite pasty story is that told by Michael Foot, scion of the famous radical westcountry family. When he deserted the tradition of Liberalism set by his father, Sir Isaac, and contested Devonport for Labour, there was strong family opposition. When he seemed likely to win, however, his mother baked a pasty and had it handed up to him at one of his meetings as a peace-offering.

The pasty even used to have a permanent place in the alphabet of the Cornish child, which ended – as I learnt it – U V W X Y Z *hampasty.* The last 'character' here is a corruption of *ampassy,* which in turn is a version of *and per se and* or *ampersand.*

Into the making of a pasty there goes one indispensable skill. The English verb to *crimp* means 'to compress or pinch into minute parallel plaits or folds', and is chiefly applied to ribbons or to curls of hair. But in Cornwall it is pasties which are crimped. The two ends of the original circle of pastry are drawn around the contents, pressed together and given a curly 'seam', as it were, with the fingers, all with great speed and dexterity. This skill is, or it used to be, a necessary qualification for a good Cornish housewife. 'Can she crimp a pasty?', or simply 'Can she crimp?', was the question a mother asked about her future daughter-in-law. With this gift, it was assumed everything else would follow.

PLAN

'Every Sunday I was planned. Sometimes I had to walk twenty miles or more, and speak three times.'

This is Billy Bray – 'the over-rated Billy Bray' as the leading authority on Cornish Methodism, the Reverend Thomas Shaw of Manchester, calls him. The use of the noun *plan*, from which Billy Bray's verb comes, is defined in 1905 in the *EDD* as: 'The annual arrangement for providing Methodist or Bible Christian preachers in the several circuits.' The editor might have added, 'the document which publishes this arrangement'. While plans are still familiar to all Methodists, the more elaborate plans were essentially rural documents; blue-prints for chapel arrangements in a wide circuit that contained too many 'wayside Bethels' to be visited frequently by a paid clergyman.

The older plans were often issued quarterly for a penny or two, and really had a plan-like appearance, opening out again and again like a map and divided vertically by Sunday date and horizontally by chapel. Abbreviations like CA, HF, SPP (Chapel Anniversary, Harvest Festival, Service of Prayer and Praise) told their own tale, but good local knowledge was called for to decide if the preacher was likely to be *handsome, bravish* or *wisht*.

On the back of the plan were the names and addresses of ministers, circuit stewards etc, with a full list of local preachers in chronological order of their 'passing up' (some had qualified for half a century) followed by a list of those 'on trial'. In the minutes of the Tenth Bible Christian Conference of 1828, under the name of William Bray there is the moving foot-note: 'Brother Bray remains on trial *at his own request*.' Such humility was rare among local preachers: 'People do say to me,' one lady preacher confided from the pulpit, '"Mrs S——, I don't know how you can get up there and speak like you do." "My friends," I do say to them, "we read in Proverbs that the wicked flee where no man pursueth, but the righteous are as bold as a lion." And then I do bear in mind that word of the Psalmist of old, when he said, "Open your mouth and I will fill it." '

In his book *Midst Mine and Moor and Cornish Folk* J. O. Keen paid tribute to the Cornishman's gift for being an attentive listener: 'They compel you to preach by the spell of their listening,' he writes, 'the sympathy is so abounding between the pulpit and the pew that preaching is a luxury there.' In return, the preacher was expected to enter into his sermon wholeheartedly. For this Father Walke of St Hilary was admired: 'A proper preacher . . . He do sweat like a bull and no mistake. Suit us all right he would, if he'd give up his old Mass, as he do call it.' Considering such exacting standards, one begins to understand why sums were set aside at Bible Christian Conferences for what was called The Worn-out Preachers' Fund.

One early plan now on permanent exhibition is that in the chapel of Tolpuddle, Dorset, for 1829; it was a measure of the monstrous nature of the court's judgment that two of the Martyrs were of sufficient standing to be 'local preachers'. Finally, it used to be said of a certain courting couple in Roche that they were so innocent they would sit hand in hand by the hour, reading the plan.

PLANCHING

Richard Carew, in his *Survey of Cornwall* (1602), contrasted the improved architecture of his day with the earlier time when men had 'covered their planchings with earth'. *Planching* obviously owes something to French *plancher*, 'a floor', or at least to French *planche*, 'a plank', though the meaning now is collective – not a single plank but a wooden floor made of several. In *Notes and Queries* for 1871 this dramatic item from a Cornish source occurs, illustrating a curious old superstition:

Mary Ann D. was taking a cup of tea wi' me, and I sez to her, 'How should granny be so long a-dyin?' And all of a sudden I screeched to Mary Ann, 'Why how can her die? Granny's athirt the planchin!' 'Good me!' sez she; and then

91

she and I tore over stairs and lashed round the bed, and all
to once granny give one groan and died direckly. She were
athirt the planchin, and couldn't die till we put her right
along it.

The word *planche* for 'a plank' is rarer and perhaps now
obsolete, but this quotation of 1892, from Sarah Hewett, is
interesting on more than linguistic grounds: 'Us du think
ourzels mortal fine now us 'ave got planche floors all dru the
house.'

Seemingly there are other Gallicisms. A habit that is
reminiscent of French is the westcountry one of saying
'Please?', corresponding closely to '(S'il vous) Plait?', instead
of standard English '(I beg your) Pardon?'. 'Don't say what,
say please,' is supposed to be advice given by Cornish mothers
on this point when training their children in manners. This
usage is not in the *EDD*. Two other instances of French
influence are the pronunciation of *biscuit* in a way closer to
French, as *biskey*, and 'singing out *morblue*', meaning 'screeching and screaming' (French *mort bleu* is euphemistic for *mort
Dieu,* 'God's death'). We must, of course, remember the
likelihood of seaboard contact with the French, as well as the
ten thousand French prisoners in Princetown in Napoleonic
times.

PUSSIVANTING

Sir Arthur Quiller-Couch's story *The Astonishing History of
Troy Town,* first published in 1888, is still very readable and,
as its frequent re-publication indicates, still read. Nor does
it detract from the interest that Q sometimes adds a footnote
about the dialect in his characters' conversation, as when he
defines *pussivanting* with these words:

I cannot forbear to add a note on this eminently Trojan
word. In the fifteenth century, so high was the spirit of the
Trojan sea-captains, and so heavy the toll of black-mail they
levied on ships of other ports, that King Edward IV sent
poursuivant after poursuivant to threaten his displeasure.
The messengers had their ears slit for their pains; and
poursuivanting or *pussivanting* survives as a term for in-
effective bustle.

Though Q's account of 'Troy' (Fowey) piracy is absolutely true, this is perhaps too parochial a way of accounting for the widespread occurrence of the word all over Devon and Cornwall. Seventeenth-century visitations of the South West by poursuivants from the College of Heralds, inquiring into entitlement to bear arms, may also be partly responsible. Yet at least there is more than a grain of truth in the attitude the word reveals. Westcountry people have never been impressed by officials and bureaucrats from Westminster.

In choosing Troy Town as a soubriquet for Fowey, Q, as so often, was adapting a dialect phrase. Troy and Fowey, of course, rhyme. We can compare the mid-Cornwall pronunciation of *mowhay* (stackyard) rhyming with *boy* and *going* rhyming with *coin*. On Tudor and Stuart maps the spelling *Foye* already indicates present-day pronunciation. *Troy Town* (originally the name in the dialect phrase referred to Priam's Troy, another surprising instance of classical knowledge percolating down into dialect) is one of two proverbially untidy places in the South West. The other is Launceston (pronounced 'Lanson') Jail, now tidied up as part of Launceston Castle and one of the sights of the South West. It lived up to its reputation when, in 1656, George Fox, founder of the Quakers, was imprisoned in a small and filthy part of it called Doomsdale, which can still be seen.

PUT AND TAKE

Put and *take* are two of our commonest English words and, used with particles, they give rise to numerous idiomatic phrasal verbs: *put out, put in for, put by, take in* etc. In dialect, however, there are also special usages of these two verbs. Perhaps the most interesting is the Cornish use of *put* in the sense of 'to escort', as in the *EDD* quotation 'He put the maid over to Camborne to see the menagerie.' The interest here is that the regular Cornish word for 'to put', *gor(r)a*, is used with the same meaning of 'to escort'. In the *Bewnans Meriasek*, when Constantine embraces Christianity he shows his respect for the Pope by attending him to his palace:

The crist ihesu ingrassaff
ha thys seluester nefra
theth palys lemen manaff
gans procescyon *gora*

And to Christ Jesu I will give thanks
And to thee Silvester ever
To thy palace now will I
With a procession *put* thee.

Standard English would have *take,* not *put,* here.

There are idiomatic dialect idioms with *take* also. The use of *take and* before a verb, to give extra force to a command, is not confined to the South West, though it is very common there. In his life of R. S. Hawker the Reverend Baring-Gould illustrates the parlous state of the church in the 1830s with this North Devon dialogue between Bishop Phillpotts and the fox-hunting parson, Mr Radcliffe:

'Mr Radcliffe, I hear, but I can hardly believe it, that men fight in your house.'
'Lor', my dear, doant 'ee believe it. When they begin fighting, I take and turn 'em out into the churchyard!'

In the westcountry I once saw a restaurant and delicatessen shop named 'Take'n Taste', but such humorous use of dialect in nomenclature is rare, not often going beyond the now somewhat hackneyed house-name 'Yertiz'. ('"Yertiz" idn' yer no more' is said to be the way a new occupant of an address returned to the GPO a letter sent to the previous owner, whose house name had been discontinued.)

QUAILAWAY

In the 1840s – I rely for this anecdote on a volume of essays *From a Cornish Window,* by Q – when the potato blight first appeared in England, an old farmer in the Duchy found this warning in his favourite almanac at the head of the page for August: 'And potentates shall tremble and quail.' Now to *quail* in Cornwall still carries its old meaning of 'to shrink, to wither' ('The braunch once dead, the budde eke needes must quaile', writes Spenser). The upshot of the prophecy was that the farmer dug his potatoes with all speed and next year the almanac was richer by a score of subscribers!

A *quailaway*, in Devon and Cornwall, is a stye on the eyelid.

RATTLE-CUM-SKIT

The sleeping habits of neighbours in villages are known and discussed. Some Cornishmen are criticised for going early to bed: 'goin bed dinner-time' (pronounce *bed* as *bayed*); on the other hand, there are those who stay up till all hours: 'proper night-crows; rattle-cum-skit by night and sleep by day'. *Rattle-cum-skit* (West Cornwall *rattle-cum-stave*) means a rumpus or a row.

Night-crows is pronounced *night-craws*, but, as so often, the word is dying out rather than becoming adapted to standard pronunciation. This pronunciation of *crow* as *craw*, *load* as *laud*, *boat* as *bought* etc, was Chaucer's pronunciation also. Dialect rhymes bear witness to it, such as this impolite one which is used when someone who does not hear clearly asks for a repeated remark with 'Eh?' instead of the more polite 'Pardon?' or (dialectal) 'Please?':

> 'Ay (ie *hay*) – straw!
> Pick yer ears and then you'll knaw.

An altogether better context to illustrate the same point is from one stanza of the lovely St Day carol, taken down as sung at St Day, near Redruth, by Mr Thomas Beard:

> Oh the holly bears a berry,
> As black as the coal;
> And Mary bore Jesus,
> Who died for us all.

There is another word *crow*, pronounced similarly. This word, however, is Celtic Cornish, not English. One can describe an untidy place as 'a proper pigs' crow', ie a pigsty. A variant was *crowdie*. The eighteenth-century diary of William Bagshaw Stevens, recently published, relates how an old Cornish woman, when asked by a judge to define the word *crowdie,* told his lordship that it was 'a little cooped-up place where we keeps a pig – just such a place as you be in, my lord'.

REAM

The radio programme was 'Down Your Way' from (I think) Looe, and a detailed description of the making of Cornish cream was underway: 'If there's a good ream on the milk . . .' 'You mean cream,' said the interviewer, interrupting. There was a stony silence. I hope he got the black looks he deserved. His informant did not, of course, mean cream. There is now some confusion of usage but generally in the South West *ream* – an Old English word, much earlier than the French loan, cream – means cream before it is scalded or clotted. If the *ream,* or *raw-ream,* is skimmed off it *reams up,* that is, it wrinkles and puckers, but not in the same way, or as thickly, as cream. Milk as it comes from the cow, ream and all, is *raw milk.* Heated or scalded (not, on any account, boiled) on a slow heat, the ream yields cream and what is left is *scald milk.* 'Is that the raw or the scald?' is still a frequent and important question on many Cornish smallholdings.

There is also a quite different south-western dialect verb to *ream,* meaning 'to stretch oneself', often used of stretching and yawning on first waking up. Writing from London to his sister Elizabeth at Bodmin on 19 February 1792, William Clift narrates how he 'went to Greenwich by land (which served to raim my legs a bit).' There may be some confusion of the two words *ream* when a young calf is said on rising up, to 'ream itself', that is, to stretch itself so that its skin gets wrinkled all over its back – a healthy sign. 'I like to see 'um ream theirselves,' says the farmer.

In a recent book entitled *British Tastes* the author notes with some surprise that 'in parts of Cornwall . . . almost all families, regardless of income, buy a quarter to half a pound of the local clotted cream each week – or, alternatively, make their own – without the slightest feeling of extravagance.' No one who knows Cornwall would question this. Cream is not a luxury but a necessity in the Duchy. Many people serve it with turnips or runner beans; with anything, in fact, except pilchards: 'cream on pilchards' is a metaphor for something overdone, in bad taste.

In both the World Wars Cornish and Devon cream were pronounced illegal. Imagine the fuss if Yorkshire pudding had been declared illegal! But why should we complain at a chance to indulge a centuries-long taste for smuggling? I have carried literally pounds of cream, all told, in a gas-mask carrier. The Cornish thoroughly enjoyed the black market; it was not patriotic, perhaps, but then neither was smuggling during the now romanticised Napoleonic wars and there are 'museums' full of exhibits purporting to be from that period up and down our coasts. Instead of watching the wall while the gentlemen went by, people were expected to turn a deaf ear to the *scritch* of pig-killing by night.

SAM-SOODLED

When I first wrote on this word, it occasioned quite a correspondence in *The Western Morning News*. Variant forms offered were *zam-zawd, zam-zoodled* and *sam-sodden*. The variation in the rendering of the spelling well illustrates the problem that bedevils all writers on dialect; how to represent in writing the sounds one hears without rendering their meaning unintelligible. The word will probably be heard, elsewhere than in West Cornwall, as if spelt with a 'z', but the spelling in 's' best shows the connection with the two root words it represents. *Soodled* is an old past participle (*sodden* is more orthodox) of the verb *seethe*. *Seethe,* meaning 'to boil', is one of the few words to do with cooking not borrowed from French but going back to OE seoþan. Now, however, the word is more often used of our tempers than of our dinners, as in 'I was seething'.

The prefix *sam-* is a native Anglo-Saxon word originally meaning 'half', rather like the Latin *semi-,* but so long disused that even in Shakespeare's day its import was not fully understood. Shakespeare describes a character in *The Merchant of*

Venice as *sand-blind,* ie 'half-blind' most probably, but the spelling shows that the meaning of 'half' had been forgotten. It has been forgotten, too, in the South West, and from the meaning of 'half-cooked' we arrive at its opposite, 'over-cooked': 'Hurry up. I've had to leave your dinner in the oven; 'twill be all sam-soodled.'

SCAT

The upland hamlet of Tregonetha, near St Columb Major, has a reputation for dilatoriness that has made its name a byword: 'like Tregonetha band, three scats behind' – *scat* here signifying a blow or a beat. As a verb *scat* means 'to hit' or 'to break', or 'to be broken', with *scat abroad* and *scat up* to represent stages in the process of disintegration. *Scat all to jowds* was once heard, meaning 'broken to pieces' or 'to smithereens'. It is even possible, by Celtic hyperbole, to 'scat your sides with laughing'.

What is left when crockery is *scat up* is called *sherds,* more commonly, in standard English, *potsherds.* Anyone not 'in the know', however, would hardly be enlightened by a definition of *sherds* I once heard: 'Sherds? Why, everybody do knaw what sherds is. Sherds is scat-up cloam!'

Scat also means to go bankrupt, or to be 'broke', as we say colloquially. In the inter-war years of agricultural depression it was said that many farmers were tempted to break off the well-known harvest hymn at 'We plough the fields and *scat——*'.

SCRUFF

Until I was at least twenty-five, I kept discovering that certain words I used regularly were not English at all, but dialect. *Teasy,* for instance, meaning 'bad-tempered', is barely standard English; neither is *lipsy,* meaning unable to sound one's 's's properly and pronouncing the sound of *th* instead. *Lisp* as a verb, of course, is common enough in standard English: 'I lisped in numbers, for the numbers came,' wrote Pope, boasting his early skill in poetry. The *OED,* however, quotes only one example of a nonce-word *lispy* and none of our metathesised *lipsy*, which, nevertheless, is illustrated in the *EDD* from Cornwall and Somerset.

Another word which I was surprised to find was not standard English was the synonym *nail-spring* for standard English 'hangnail' – a small piece of cuticle, partially detached, at one end of, or near, a finger-nail. Nor was it standard English to refer to an oilskin waterproof coat as an *oiler*, nor to a circular bread roll as a *split*, nor to a cobbler's waxed thread as a *wax end*. In standard English people did not speak of *trolling* their feet when they twisted or turned them, or walked otherwise than on the ball of the foot; nor, when shoes pinched them, did they say, 'these shoes *draw* my feet'; nor, though the remedy might be effective, did they talk of '*pitching* on the cold *canvas*' for bearing the weight of the foot on cold linoleum when they had cramp in the toe.

One dialect verb that standard English could well use is to *scruff*. Not in the *OED*, it is defined in the *EDD* as 'to struggle and fight' or 'to lay hold of and pull about'. These definitions seem to me to miss the point of to *scruff*, which nowadays, at least, means to do such things in play or in fun. The English equivalent is 'horseplay', a noun on the same lines, but which smacks of Dr Arnold and sounds disapproving. 'Sparring' will not do; it is too professional, implying too much compliance with Queensberry rules. Fighting, in Cornwall, whether in play or in earnest, does not immediately descend to fisticuffs. There are technical terms like *foreheap* and *foretrip*, *forehitch* and *flying mare*, which testify to the importance of *the Cornish hug*. There is also the less reputable verb to *faggoty* – from the idea of being bound together as in a faggot – meaning 'to sell one's back in *wrassling*', that is, to combine together and bargain not to win. Shakespeare had a pronunciation of *wrassle* very like our own, as the spelling of the First Folio edition confirms: 'It is yong Orlando, that tript vp the Wrastlers heeles, and your heart, both in an instant.'

SHINER

This word is a good deal commoner in Cornwall than in standard English, with more varied meanings than the usual colloquial one of a black eye. Mr Tom Tremewan recalls in *Cornish Youth* that he worked as assistant to some masons on leaving school, and from them he learnt not to lay stones with their thickest end outwards. Such stones were known as *shiners* and were considered a sign of bad workmanship. I looked in vain for this word in the dialect glossaries and dictionaries until, in the *OED* supplement, I came upon this single quotation from a South African book on ostrich farming: 'The great thing to look out for is that the men do not put in shiners – that is, stones showing their longest faces to the front.' It seems that westcountrymen have carried standards of workmanship, and the terminology to assert them, all over the world.

There is another, and more general, meaning of this word in the South West. It occurs both as a vocative ('my old shiner') and in general with the meaning of a sweetheart, though I doubt if either *shiner* for 'sweetheart', or *sparking* (of the same vintage) for 'courting' are much used now. Occasionally 'Shiner' still occurs as a nickname, with suggestions of a lively fellow, or even a dandy – the kind that was widely called by the American importation, *masher*, in the last decades of the nineteenth century. I quote from a short-story in *Longman's Magazine* (1893):

> Charlie . . . with a red rose in his button-hole matching the one in Martha's bonnet. His hat stuck so much on one side that it almost hung on his ear – a sure sign a young man is trying to look a 'shiner' *anglice* 'masher' . . .

SLIGHT

Some time in the late nineteenth century the following conversation occurred in West Cornwall and was reported by Miss Courtney:

'Your daughter looks well.'
'No, she's but *slight*; her face is her best *limb*.'

Only rarely can such a casual remark have travelled so far. It was printed by Wright in the *EDD* and taken from there by the editors of the *OED*. In standard English, of course, *limbs* are parts of the body distinct from the head and trunk, this West Cornwall usage, of a more central part of the body, having been dead in the standard language for centuries. I doubt if it will be heard now, even in West Cornwall, though Mrs Kathleen Hawke records having heard it in the West, in her admirable, but as yet unpublished dialect glossary.

What is still heard is *limb* in the sense of a mischievous person; while its 'toned-down' use, for mischievous children, is so widespread as not to be dialectal at all. 'He's a proper limb' is often said in the West in pride rather than in anger, and formerly, a common phrase was 'an anointed limb'. The idea is of 'a *limb* of Satan' and is a very old notion in both English and Cornish. A boy from Camborne is described in the *Bewnans Meriasek* with the words '*esel* yv then tebel el' – 'a limb he is of the evil angel'.

Slight for 'unwell' in the opening quotation is still often heard; my grandparents spoke, rather contradictorily, of people being 'fine and slight' or 'fine and poorly'. There is a special westcountry verb meaning 'to moan constantly about illness'; this is *creening* (also *creening up*). There are also two phrases which give short shrift to the hypochondriac:

'What's the matter with her?'
'Oh, a flea kicked her. Only a fart doubled up, that's all.'

Most of the 'complaints' Canon Hammond enumerated in 1897 are still comprehensible dialect words, particularly in the St Austell area where his parish was: "'E's pinickin, palchy and totelish, clicky and cloppy and a kiddles and quaddles all day.' ('He's puny, weakly and his mind is wandering, left-handed and lame and he dawdles and grumbles all day.')

SLIPPER

Slippery is the standard English equivalent of this word while *slippy* is the Midlands and northern variant, but the south-western word has the best pedigree of the three. The Old English word was *slipor*, and *slippery* seems not to have been recorded in English until Coverdale's version of the Old Testament in 1545; *slippy* first appears, according to the *OED*, a few years later. Before that time icy roads all over England were probably said to be *slipper* (now pronounced, in broad dialect, *slepper*), as they still are in the South West.

The word has literal and figurative ramifications which can be differentiated by appropriate comparisons. Icy roads, for instance, are 'slipper's glass' or 'like a glass bottle'; whereas people who are slippery customers (in *Othello* Iago describes Cassio as 'a slipper and subtle knave') are said to be 'slipper's a eel'. 'Slipper as *an* eel' is not heard in pure dialect; the indefinite article before vowels is elided, as is the definite article. This sort of elision was commoner in earlier standard English, a pronunciation reflected, for example, in George Herbert's hymn:

> Who sweeps a room as for Thy laws
> Makes that and th' action fine.

SLOCK

When I began teaching, I was told by a Cornish schoolmaster of many years' experience, and who, unlike many westcountry schoolmasters, was too intelligent to despise dialect, 'Boy, there's two sorts of teachers: there's drivers and there's *slockers*. The drivers make more row but the slockers do do best in the long run.'

It will be a pity if this south-western dialect word – found in Cornwall, Devon, Somerset, Hampshire and Pembroke-shire, according to the *EDD* – were to die out. It means 'to lure, entice, or decoy', from an Old French verb *esloquer,* and it is one of several words that Carew employs, as in this description of an attempted seduction from his translation of Tasso's

Godfrey of Bulloigne: 'In vaine she sought to slocke, or with mortall sweetnings t'enroll him in Cupidos pay.' A *slocker* is not only a person but also a lure or bait that entices. Thus the word can be a dialect term for what Victorian tradesmen called *sacrifices* and the manager of a modern supermarket calls a *loss leader*.

This use of the suffix *-er* to describe things, as well as persons, is dialectal. A local tradesman once told me that he went to do an odd job at the house of a woman of substance and probity, but who was also notoriously 'difficult'; 'She left a sixpence lying on the table; but I knawed 'nuff not to take that; I thought to myself: "That's the bloody *tester!*"' A notice formerly to be seen on some Cornish beaches which must have amused visitors was 'Do not sit in deck-chairs with wet *bathers*'!

SMEECH

'You "slow and sure" folks be just like a faggot o' green furze 'pon the fire.' (Daniel Quorm is castigating luke-warm Methodists), 'You don't blaze nor burn; you . . . go fillin' the house with smeech and smoke.' *Smoke* is from OE *smoca* and *smeech* from OE *smec*. The two words are not identical in meaning in the south-western dialect, though it seems they were to the Anglo-Saxon translator of Psalm 102:3, who writes *smece gelice* for 'like smoke' in 'My days are consumed like smoke'. Only *smoke* survives in standard English, but in the South West *smeech* means 'the smell of burning, the smell or taste of smoke, any dust or obscurity in the air'. I remember a westcountry voice protesting, 'What a smeech!' as smoke came into a railway carriage through an open window when going through a tunnel near Liskeard.

Two more interesting dialect variants for standard English words are *doust* beside the normally short-vowelled *dust,* and *croust* beside *crust*. *Doust* is a special kind of dust, the refuse thrown or raked out (unenviable job) from winnowing or threshing; and *croust* is a special form of crust, a snack taken afield. When, during the war, I went 'picking potatoes' in the Penzance area, I soon learnt the welcome call of

'Croust-time!' In mid-Cornwall one is more likely to hear *crib* or *crib-time*, although *crib* is perhaps industrial rather than agricultural. In *Cornish Youth* Mr Tremewan speaks, as a Perranporth man, of *croust* in the harvest field and the *crib* for which, as *kiddle-boy* to a gang of masons working on the railway, he had to boil the tea. Another word for a mid-morning snack, heard occasionally in both Devon and Cornwall, is a *levener*, for what is elsewhere called 'elevenses'.

SNOBBY-NOSED

An interesting switch of meaning occurs between south-western dialect and standard English with the two words *snob* and *snot*. In Devon and Cornwall the former means 'mucus from the nose' and the latter is 'a conceited, haughty person', with the adjectives *snobby*, as in *snobby-nosed*, and *snotty*, meaning 'stuck up', corresponding.

Writing about this transference in *The Western Morning News*, I asked how the word *snotty* as a slang term for a midshipman had come about. By return of post I received two letters, one from a Vice-Admiral and one from a Rear-Admiral, both volunteering the information that the word *snotty* for a midshipman was probably due to the midshipman's alleged tendency to wipe his nose on his sleeve. The three buttons on the cuff of the midshipman's round jacket were said to be put there to discourage this habit!

SPARROWBILL

In standard English we probably associate the word *tap* with the heel of a boot or shoe rather than the sole; partly owing to the derived connection of 'heeltaps' with the remnants of liquor left in a glass. Dialectally, however, the *tap* is more often the sole of a shoe, and to *tap boots* usually means 'to re-sole' them. Perhaps coincidentally, but more probably as a borrowing from provincial English, a South Wales equivalent of *tapping boots* is *tapo 'sgidiau*. The verb in this meaning has also crosssed the Atlantic.

I knew at least one Cornishman who economised on his economies by getting the rubber to repair the soles of shoes from beating out old bicycle tyres found at a neighbouring dump. More orthodox materials for tapping boots were rather specialised. In mid-Cornwall *sprigs* and *tingles* were the respective names of the round and square-shanked tacks to secure the leather. *Sprigs* had more head on them than *tingles*. *Hobs* and *studs* were the square-headed and round-headed massive nails with short shanks that were driven into the soles of heavy boots to protect them.

Another, more general, name for boot-tacks with little or no heads is *sparrowbills*. There is a lane in Truro called Sparrable Lane – *sparrable* being a variant of *sparrowbill* – perhaps so named from the sharp stones which the feet encountered there.

In the *EDD*, Wright gives an amusing expression for someone with a large appetite: 'She do ate like a gurt gannet and can clunk sparrowbill pie.' An equivalent hyperbole is 'She'll eat a horse and chase the rider.'

STAGGED

He that will not happy be
With a pretty girl by the fire,
I wish he were 'pon tap o' Dartmoor,
A-stagged in the mire.

Stagged means 'stuck in the mud', either literally or in the metaphorical sense of being behindhand with work and cumbered with much serving. 'Stagged like a pig in shit' is a usual comparison. *Lagged* is used of clothing and means 'bedraggled in the mud' – *dabbered up*, as is also said. This meaning of *lagged* was known to writers in more central parts of England, such as Bunyan: 'Let your new garments not lag with dust and dirt.'

STANK

To stank means 'to trample or stamp'. Mr Tremewan quotes a local preacher's description of St Paul's meeting with

Ananias after being blinded on the road to Damascus. The apostle, said the preacher, came in very quietly, 'no hobby boots, no stanking about'. A local grave-digger, I remember, was not so considerate. He stamped on the earth as he filled in the new grave of a clay-captain: 'I said to myself, "You been on top of me pretty many times, Cap'n, but I'm on top of you now," and I stanked 'un down!' This is another Celtic Cornish word.

A word with slightly different meaning is to *stram*, meaning 'to stride'. It is frequently used in the phrase 'stramming along like anybody pacing tatie-ground', ie ground which has been planted with potatoes, necessitating big strides between the rows that are 'banked up'. "Tis no good for 'ee to bring no up-the-country piece down here,' an old-style Cornish woman is said to have told her son who had gone away to be educated and was in danger of matrimony, 'Here be we stramming through with the pigs' pail in our hand!'

STICKLER

A *stickler* now means, in standard English, 'one who stands upon points', who insists pertinaciously on some principle, ceremony etc. In the South West, the earlier meaning of 'an umpire' is still heard, especially in *wrasslin* circles. Shakespeare knew this meaning too:

> The dragon wing of night o'erspreads the earth
> And, stickler-like, the armies separates.

Another instance of dialect differentiation is the word *tab* which, besides meaning, as in standard English, 'an attachment for pulling, a tag', has also in Devon and Cornwall the sense of a piece of turf with grass attached: 'I catched up a tab and thrawed at 'un.'

Sometimes a word changes not only its meaning, but also its grammatical function, in the dialect. Thus in the South West the word *frail* is not only an adjective meaning, as in standard English 'feeble', but also a noun, meaning 'a limp bag or basket, made of straw or cloth, for carrying fruit, vegetables etc.' Jeremiah (24:2) had a vision in which he was shown two baskets; in the King James Bible this is rendered thus: 'One basket had very good figs . . . and the other basket had very naughty figs.' In the earlier Wycliff version, the word for basket is *fraiel*: 'And oe fraiel hadde good figus . . . and the oe fraiel hadde euele figis.' This word now tends to be dialectal, being rarely heard in the North, as a westcountryman found when he inquired at a Mersey-side lost-property office, having left his *frail* on the train.

Another instance of changed grammatical function is the word *keenly*, which is more often an adjective in the South West than an adverb. It means 'capable', or 'promising', as in 'She's some good maid to work; some keenly 'bout the house.' A promising vein of ore used to be described as 'a brave keenly lode'. *Binch* (bench) can occur as a verb in an interesting usage that has nevertheless escaped the *EDD*; only the past participle *binched* is found, and the meaning is literally 'stuck on a bench', used to mean 'remaining as an unwelcome guest': 'She's binched for th'evening.' Such people are accused of *housing*, that is, going visiting from house to house. Finally, *cabby* is less a rather old-fashioned name for a cab- or taxi-driver, than the adjective, 'dirty, slovenly'. To *cab* is to mishandle or to handle in a messy way: 'If you don't want that food, don't cab it up,' or 'Don't cab the cat.'

STIDDLE

I quoted in the Introduction the complaint of an old Cornish farmer that younger farm-workers could no longer tell a *stiddle* from a *staddle*. Many middle-aged westcountrymen would doubtless know both words. A *stiddle*, or *studdle*, is a post. In mining terms, it would be something like a pit-prop; in farming, a post to which cattle are tethered in a cow-shed. *Staddles* have deteriorated recently from folk-life to folksiness; they are those stone 'toadstools', much in demand as garden ornaments in suburbia. Originally they formed the stands on which ricks of unthreshed corn rested, and they had the far from ornamental purpose of preventing rats from climbing up into the stacks. In some parts of the West, the *staddle* means the whole foundation or framework on which a rick is built. This word may survive, if only because it appears in a poem, 'The Child and the Mowers', by that most undervalued of poets, William Barnes of Dorset:

> Then they took en in hwome to his bed,
> An' he rose vrom his pillow no mwore.
> Vor the curls on his sleek little head
> To be blown by the wind out o' door.
> Vor he died while the hay russled grey
> On the staddle so leately begun:
> Lik' the mown-grass a-dried by the day –
> Aye! the zwath-flow'r's a-kill'd by the zun.

In mid-Cornwall this framework or foundation is often called a *stead* (diphthong as in *great*).

But perhaps we should not stop at distinguishing *stiddles* from *staddles*. What else might the elderly countrymen accuse us of not knowing? Will the hedge-trimmer, with his modern-day machines for paring hedges, soon not know a reaping-hook (sickle-shaped) from what is called in Devon and Cornwall a *patch-hook,* that is, a 'bill-hook'? Does the modern clay-worker need to distinguish between a pick and a *dubber*? Is the present-day farmer sure that he can tell a *biddix* from a *vizgy* (twybill), and either from a *two-clawed hacker*?

Specimens of these and other tools are now only to be found in museums such as the Sticklepath Museum of Rural Industry near Okehampton, on the main A30 road. Here the Finch Foundry Trust displays implements made by the foundry from 1814 to 1960. 'Trip' hammers, fans and grinding wheels are still in action, powered by water from the River Taw.

STOCKING-NIDDLES

'One of these days I hope to write a treatise on the Mayors of Cornwall,' wrote Q in *Noughts and Crosses,* 'dignitaries whose pleasant fame is now night, remembered only in some neat byword or saying of the country people. Thus you may hear, now and again, of "The Mayor of Falmouth, who thanked God when the town jail was enlarged", "The Mayor of Market Jew, sitting in his own light", or "the Mayor of

Calenich, who walked two miles to ride one".' Unhappily, as far as I know, Q did not write his 'treatise', and the phrases by which these gentlemen are remembered will soon be entirely forgotten. Sometimes this frequent introduction into dialect speech of such mayoral and other personages of minor fame seems, at first, gratuitous. The full story must be known to throw light on the situation for which the phrase is appropriate. Canon Hammond explains why St Austell people drag in the phrase 'like John Tregonning's pig' after criticising someone for having 'a short memory': 'John Tregonning used to tell how he had boiled some potatoes for the "peg" and served them up hot. The pig dropped one which he found too warm for him with great alacrity, but the next moment returned to the same potato again.'

It will often be found that bywords and metaphorical adages, far from being roundabout, represent a sort of shorthand, saving the speaker what would otherwise be quite elaborate descriptions of situations. The magazine *Old Cornwall* quotes this phrase: 'like some helpers, pulling down with a bar ire (iron bar), and propping up with a stocking-niddle.' We can all recognise the type of assistance indicated, from this brief figurative description.

But a word like *stocking-niddle* reminds us that these similes are bound to lose force with changing times. Now that people do not knit stockings and socks so frequently (the word *stocking* generally covered both in the dialect – one gentleman of my acquaintance rejoiced in the nickname of 'Buggering Stockens' from an exclamation he uttered when he had lost his football socks), a phrase like 'eyes flashing like stocking-niddles' is less vivid. So, too, comparing staring eyes to *chapel hat-pegs* means less, not merely because there are fewer chapel-goers and fewer hats, but also because modern hat-pegs are generally mass-produced metal objects. To realise the full impact of the phrase we need to go somewhere like Polbrock, where the hillside chapel, high on the wooded slopes above a tributary of the River Camel, has a full set of wooden hat-pegs, hand-turned, with round heads, and sticking out about nine inches from the wall.

STROIL

There is sometimes remarkable unity of dialect throughout the South West. 'What do you call this?' asks the *SED* field-worker, holding up some couch-grass. 'Stroil' is the answer throughout Cornwall, Devon and Somerset. The word sounds as horrible as the weed is. Or again, to the question, 'What do some workmen wear below their knees to lift the trouser-leg up (to prevent it being *lagged* with mud)?' the almost unanimous answer from Wiltshire, Somerset, Devon and Cornwall ten years ago was *yorks*. There was still wider agreement, as far east as Sussex, about what to call 'those dark blue berries the size of a pea, growing on a low plant on the moors'. *Hurts* or *whorts* is the regular southern dialect abbreviation of *whortleberries*.

The trick in asking such questions, it will be obvious from these examples, is not to put a word into a dialect speaker's mouth. Like poetry for Keats, the word must come as naturally as leaves to a tree, or it had better not come at all.

It is also worth noting that some words do not occur in the dialect of the South West at all. As a boy I never really knew what bracken was, for the word is hardly used in Devon and Cornwall, where *ferns*, or in broader dialect *vearns*, covers both 'ferns' and 'bracken'. Hardly anybody speaks, either, of *retching* or *reaching* before being sick; people do not *retch*, they *urge*. Dr Wakelin, however, thinks that *retch* and *urge* may well be the same word, with the sound 'r' transposed or metathesised.

This transposition of 'r' is quite common in various English dialects. In Cornwall an *apron* is often called an *apern*, and still more characteristically *saffron* is *saffern* and *groaty-meat* – made from pigs' innards, spice and groats – is *gurty-meat*.

STRUB

Some words that are fast disappearing from the South West are *davered*, used of flowers that are faded, *muffly* or *murfly*, meaning 'freckled', and *brackety* or *braggoty*, meaning 'speckled', often used of marks on a newborn baby – 'A brackety chield is a healthy chield' was the proverb. *Brackety* is of Celtic origin (compare Irish *brecc*, Welsh *brych*, 'a spot') and is one of the few such words still heard outside West Cornwall. The late 'Cap'n' Marshel Arthur quotes an advertisement once 'cried' from the 'crying stone' in the churchyard at St Stephen-in-Brannel:

> A goose and a gander
> From Carloggan did wander.
> The goose is brackety
> The gander white,
> Been gone a fortnit
> And bain't back yit.

I doubt whether the younger generation know any of these words; yet, like Charles II, they are an unconscionable time a-dying. *Davered* was recorded in *Notes and Queries* of 1854 for fear it should be lost, and not many years later, in 1870, a Cornishman wrote to the same journal about two words that he thought would shortly be extinct; *mort*, meaning lard or pig's fat melted down, and the verb to *strub* birds' nests, meaning 'to strip or rob' them. Private individuals, if not public bodies, have more respect for the environment than they once had. Nowadays people don't go 'strubbing birds' nesteses' as indiscriminately as they did in Queen Victoria's day, but I shall be surprised if this word is not recalled by many westcountrymen each spring.

The verb to *mort*, from the noun mentioned above, means 'to turn to fat, to put on fat'. I remember paying a visit one Christmas Day in the afternoon and being told: 'We'm sitting here morting after our Christmas dinner.' Animals that *mort* well are said to be *good doers*: 'I'd rather have a good doer than a do-gooder any day,' one independent farmer is said to have remarked.

Returning to the last line of 'Cap'n' Arthur's advertisement, *bain't* is a curious mixed-up negative that alternates with the commoner *ain't*. In mid-Cornwall the two words tend to be pronounced *bent* and *ent* respectively. *Bain't* is very broad dialect, and rarer now, but it was not long ago that three schoolgirls were questioned suspiciously by a caretaker in Truro museum: 'You maidens bain't eatin' chips in here, be 'ee?'

STUG

'What do you call the large earthenware thing,' the tireless fieldworkers of the *SED* asked, 'in which people keep, or used to keep, their bread?' In reply there is the Devon word *stean*, which seems to have been used also for salted meat and for butter, and the West Cornwall word *bussa*. There is a hill in the Isles of Scilly called Bussa Hill. As for *stean* (OE stæn, 'an earthenware jug', related to *stone*), in the mythological figures representing the months in Spenser's *The Faerie Queene*, January is shown thus:

Upon an huge great Earth-pot steane he stood
From whose wide mouth there flowed forth the Romane Flood.

The survey also recorded, only from St Ewe although it is known more widely, the mid-Cornwall word, a *stug*. One of the most evocative scenes in the late Claude Berry's book on Cornwall is that of his grandmother, half-way through Saturday morning's housework, saying, 'My dear sawl, I'm feeling so weak as a robin', whereupon she helps herself and her grandson to either a small basin of *kiddley-broth* or a cup of tea and a slice of saffron cake out of the brown earthenware *stug*. As the dialect epitome of weakness, by the way, the robin interchanges with the wren: 'so weak as a wrannie'. Miss Courtney notes the adage:

Hurt a robin or a wran,
Never prosper, boy nor man.

In the far west, a disagreeable or monotonous song is said to be 'like a bee droning in a bussa'; in the less refined parts of the county, farther east, such a song is compared to 'a pig farting in a stug'.

SUGARY-WAD

One of my great-grandfathers went to a dame-school. So did my daughter, but hers was called a play-group. I do not think that the inspectors who come to oversee these modern 'dame-schools' would approve of an expedient much resorted to in my great-grandfather's dame-school in the moorland hamlet of Criggan, in Roche parish, 130 years ago. This was a small flour-bag filled with bread, butter and sugar, which some of the children carried and sucked constantly as a tranquiliser. Such 'trade' was known as *sugary-wad*. The 'dame' approved; she said she only wished that all children would come provided with *sugary-wad*, and indeed it does not seem to have done my great-grandfather much harm. He lived to a good age and reared what used to be called in the westcountry a *long family*.

The *wad* of *sugary-wad* was pronounced as Shakespeare pronounced it, rhyming with *bad* not with *God*. The seventeenth-century change of standard English whereby *wa* became *wo* or *waw* never occurred in the dialects of the far South West. We can contrast to *squall* (rhyme: *pal*) – a very common variant for 'to weep', as in 'I squalled my eyes out' – or *squallarse* (rhyme: *Callas*) – for what in Nottinghamshire is called a *mardarse* and in standard English a *crybaby* – with the BBC weatherman and his '*squally* (rhyme: *rawly*) showers'.

TANTARA BOBUS

All English dialects have their scraps of nonsense, as befits a country which has produced Edward Lear and Lewis Carroll. It is interesting to find a parallel to the dormouse's story in *Alice in Wonderland* of the three sisters who lived at the bottom of a treacle well, in a phrase like 'Tregonetha treacle mines'. Tregonetha, an inland hamlet, is also credited with a harbour just as it is said to be possible to 'go out Roche Rock to pick limpets', though Roche is several miles from the coast.

Certain people are constantly reminded of alleged blunders in the past with taunting questions like 'Who whipped the hake?' or 'Who shot the pig?'. Former howlers ascribed to certain egregious idiots are kept alive by repetition; like 'Murder committed, but nobody hurted,' or 'There, I knawed that pig was heavier than I thought he was!'

Two nonsensical reasons for catching a cold are said to be 'sleeping with your mouth abroad' or 'drinking out of a damp cup'. A house whose foundations are not firm is said to be 'tied to the hedge with a bramble'. The Reverend Thomas Shaw, in *A History of Cornish Methodism*, records that the wayside chapel of 'Uncle' Frank Tamblyn, between Liskeard and Bodmin, was said to be 'tied to the ground with a bramble'. The word *hedgyboor*, perhaps varied to *hadgypoor*, from being a dialect word for 'a hedghog' comes to mean any nonsensical monster. In this category, too, comes *Tantara Bobus*, half-bogey-man, half archetypal fool, whose achievements include 'living till he died', and 'getting out of bed to see if his feet was covered up'.

'TEAL'

There are certain verbs which are much more frequently used in the South West than in standard English. One such verb is *till*, pronounced as *teal* (compare *beal* for a bird's bill), which is in widespread and common use. Westcountrymen *teal* not only the garden in general, but also potatoes and even seeds. 'We do generally reckon to teal taties Good Friday.' They *sow* seeds only in hymns, usually speaking of *putting* a field *to* or *in* corn, potatoes etc.

Another such word of wide occurrence is *tell*, used where standard English varies with *speak, talk,* or *say*: 'What be 'ee telling 'bout 'tall?' ('at all' – a contemptuous addition); or 'She's always telling 'bout somebody' (ie abusing them). Reported from Devon are sentences like 'Her can talk, but her can't tell a speech yet,' referring to a small girl that can as yet say only single words. A Cornish equivalent of 'tell that to the marines' was 'tell that up in Devonshire'. As with *talk, whisper, grizzle* and *look,* the contemptuous addition of *up* is common: 'telling up a lot of old plod'.

Of fine summer evenings elderly men are often to be seen sitting on the public seat, such as you will find in most villages (one I know is referred to as 'the House of Lords'), smoking their pipes and 'telling the tale'. The best 'tales' are of the grass-roots variety. The raciness of high-spirited west-country narrative has not often been captured on paper, but here is an account from Mr Tremewan of his earliest experiences as a 'local preacher' in Probus. It will be noted that the speaker scorns a monotonous use of plain indicative statements; questions and exclamations diversify his story:

> ''Ave 'ee got any dinner?'
> 'No,' I said.
> 'Well, we don't provide no dinner here...We don't belong to give dinner to preachers . . . but you can come in and sit down.'
> I was shown into a little dark room with very old-fashioned poor furniture. Judging from the stale smell of the place I should say the room was rarely used. There I sat, thinking of the words spoken to me by my fellow-apprentices when they knew how I spent my Sundays: 'You . . . fool!' At last, breaking the silence, I heard a rushing about in the farm-yard. Then, at 'double f', 'Caw! caw! caw!' 'Dear! dear! dear!' thought I, 'that poor old rooster that I saw as I came into the yard . . . and all for me!'
> After about an hour's waiting, in came the pie! I will say a generous plateful was given me, including a leg! But tough? I chewed and chewed and chewed, but it wouldn't go down. I pretended a cough, and with my hand placed the mouthful on the side of the plate.
> You think I am exaggerating? I am not . . . I got through the two services, and on the way home in the wagonette I *told all the tale,* to the unbounded amusement of my two preacher companions.

Another verb that is very much commoner in the dialect is to *travel.* It means specifically, as it hardly does in standard English, 'to walk', not merely 'to make a journey': 'I seen her travelling with her frail down the village first thing in the morning.' To *serve* in the sense of 'to treat' is also more common. Not only can we be 'served right', we can also be 'served bad' or 'served rough': 'He served that dunkey some rough'. To *pick* occurs more widely, especially in the very frequent dialect phrase to *pick fowls,* meaning 'to pluck them'. Sarah Hewett, as so often, has just the right quotation from Devon: 'Luke sharp, Jane, and pick they vowls. Yu knaw there's zebben geeze and dree turkeys 'et tu be picked.' If poor Jane knows what she is about, she will *dip* some of 'they vowls', that is, soak them in hot water to make the picking easier. In the Sabbatarian atmosphere of early twentieth-century Cornwall children were told that the man in the moon had been sent up there for 'picking sticks on a Sunday'.

TERRIBLE

'John,' a Cornish mother proudly told me, 'is terrible with sums.' At first hearing there is something almost biblical about such a statement, recalling *The Song of Solomon*: 'Who is she that looketh forth in the morning . . . terrible as an army with banners?' But the idiom, in fact, is quite different. The meaning is that, given sums to do, John becomes (if the pun is not too painful) a figure to be reckoned with. *Terrible over* and *terrible about* also occur. The *EDD* quotes from Somerset a sentence that might well be heard farther west, 'Mr Venn's terrible over his bullocks'; meaning he is inordinately attentive to them. There are also expressions like, 'She's terrible 'bout her father'; that is, she has a depth of affection for him that is almost frightening in its intensity.

THIRL

Though all the dictionaries and glossaries are silent on the point, this word, still occasionally heard, meaning 'gaunt, thin, hollow-eyed, hungry-looking', may be connected with the OE verb *yrlian*, 'to pierce', whence *nostril* from 'nose-piercing'. 'Thirl's a greyhound' was the simile, and 'So thin that the belly and back are almost brought together' is one definition. The variant Devon form *thirdle* suggests a meta-thesised past participle, ie *thirled*.

TIFLES

Dialect, even in its present decayed state, can still spring surprises on those unfamiliar with it. There was the Yorkshire teacher who set her East Cornwall class to use the word *race* in as many different ways as possible and got back the sentence, 'The woman wore a *race* of pearls'. If *race* is ambiguous what about *runner*? For many westcountrymen, especially those connected with quarrying or mining, a *runner* means a fall of earth; for others, perhaps, an endless length of towelling on a roller behind the door. From dressmaking comes a word that must have mystified 'foreigners' working in Cornish dressmakers' shops at the turn of the century. At the end of the day the work-room would be strewn with what were called *tifles* or *tiflings* (rhyme: *trifles* or *triflings*), that is, wisps and strands of cotton. The word *tifles* is still heard in mid-Cornwall. To have a hair or a *tifle* in the mouth is said to be a sure symptom of being annoyed.

The most amusing example of a dialect misunderstanding I know occurred many years ago, in the days before milk came hygienically bottled but was delivered in jugs and measures. A young housewife from the Midlands, new to St Austell, was informed by her milkman as he brought in the milk, 'Coming in dirty, mum.' It was some time before she realised that he was not decrying his own wares but referring to the weather. The phrase 'coming in dirty' is often necessary in the South West. In one way (though holiday brochures do not dwell on the fact) nothing recalls Cornwall quite so well as the word *skiffy* – 'a little skiffy shower'. 'Light driving rain' is the definition in dialect glossaries, and we are well used to it. There is a saying, 'Cornwall will stand a shower every day, and two for Sundays.' Drought is rarely a problem; much more likely is the prospect of returning home from an outing, wet and bedraggled. This was known as a 'Mevagissey rig', defined as 'a wet arse and no fish'.

TO

Prepositions are small words, the small-change of language, and like small-change they are in constant use. Sometimes they occur in dialect where the speaker of standard English would not consider them necessary. An excellent instance is quoted in *The Dialect of West Somerset* by the Victorian dialectician, F. T. Elworthy. He quotes a man who called out at a political meeting held in Taunton on 8 November 1885, 'Where's Gordon to?' The question was not answered until the beginning of the next year, unfortunately. The extra *to* is very common. 'That's where 'tis to' means 'that is the situation', an idea also expressed with an extra *of* as in 'That's of it'. ('Who's of it?' was the question children used to ask in school playgrounds; ie 'Who is the one who is chasing the others?') *To* is often used in place of various standard English prepositions: *at*, in 'I see she was to the funeral, then'; *out of*, in 'I'll turn 'ee to doors'; *in comparison with*, in 'He is a king to his brother' and *for*, in 'There's one pasty to father and one to you'.

An extra *for* before the *to* of the infinitive is quite common still throughout the South West. Perhaps the most famous example is the reason Tom Pearse's horse was borrowed: 'I want for to go to Widecombe Fair'.

TOWZER

One rarely hears tadpoles referred to in the South West, nowadays, as *tom-totties*. Formerly if a person was suspected of being too intellectual for their own well-being, they were dismissed with the phrase 'like a tom-totty, all head and no body!' Other rhymes of criticism were 'Outward flink, inward stink', used of women who set more store by finery than personal cleanliness; or 'This is water bewitcht and tea begritcht!', for very weak or badly-made tea. Chaucer seems to have pronounced this last word rather similarly. When the heroine of *Troilus and Criseyde* finds herself in a compromising situation from which there is no escape, she decides that she may as well stay with a good grace 'as *grucche* and thanne abide'. For the change of vowel here we can compare the dialectal *tich-pipe*, for *touch-pipe*, meaning 'to break', or 'a break from work for a rest and a smoke'. (People thinking of giving up smoking might remember the Cornish proverb: 'A change of work is as good as a tich-pipe'.) We can also compare the old pronunciation of *flour-hutch* as *flour'itch*.

Ask any modern housewife, as she carries home her bag of flour from a supermarket, what a *flour-hutch* is and the chances are that she will not know, though the word is not really dialectal. Here, however, we have the reason for the disuse of many words; either the objects they represent are no longer used, or they have been given a new, perhaps a trade, name. But many of us remember the 4ft high chests, divided into two or more compartments and with sloping lids, into which were tipped half-hundredweight bags of flour for the big weekly bakings (for *boughten* cakes, besides being dear, were despised as inferior). The flourbags would be inscribed, as like as not, with the names of that most Cornish of trinities, Messrs Hosken, Trevithick and Polkinhorn – abbreviated HTP for short, but reconstituted by village wits as 'Hot turnip pasties'. These bags could be washed and bleached and then used for table-cloths, while the hessian corn sacks were made into tough aprons or wrappers for rough housework, known in some parts of Devon and Cornwall as *towzers*, but I do not suppose that anybody wears them now.

TRADE

To understand the dread implications that this word has had in English in the past one has only to take up a nineteenth-century novel – Mrs Gaskell's *Wives and Daughters* for example. In the town of Hollingford, where the story is set, there is a circulating library, but 'no shopkeeper would have thought of offering himself as a member, however great his general intelligence and love of reading'; or again, the local doctor takes two trainees into his profession, '"pupils" as they were called in the genteel language of Hollingford, "apprentices" as they were in fact'.

This was in the Midlands of course – in fact Warwickshire, described by Henry James as 'unmitigated England'. On the Celtic fringes the classes were less rigidly divided. For evidence of this, we can turn to Dr John Davy's picture of Penzance at the turn of the century, from his biography of his more famous brother, Sir Humphry:

> At that time, when our colonial possessions were very limited, our army and navy on a small scale, and there was comparatively little demand for intellect, the younger sons of gentlemen were often of necessity brought up to some trade or mechanical art, to which no discredit, or loss of caste, as it were, was attached. The eldest son, if not allowed to remain an idle country squire, was sent to Oxford or Cambridge, preparatory to his engaging in one of the three liberal professions of divinity, law or physic; the second son was perhaps apprenticed to a surgeon or apothecary, or a solicitor; the third to a pewterer or watchmaker; the fourth to a packer or mercer, and so on, were there more to be provided for . . . When settled in business, they were not excluded from what would now be considered genteel society.

If the social implications of the word *trade* were less deeply felt, however, the word has other, and wider, connotations in the South West. Again, as so often, we encounter continued south-western usage of earlier English that might seem outlandish elsewhere. In 1645 one T. Wilson, a Puritan controversialist, wrote a pamphlet entitled 'Childe's Trade; or the Beginning of the Doctrine of Christ, whereby Babes may have Milk, Children Bread Broken'. 'Leave that alone; that's the cheild's trade!' is still heard in the South West. *Trade* thus becomes a very useful generalising term; it can even occur as a generalising suffix. When told that he was being given a present, a young friend of mine, very much in the ancient mould, asked, 'Is it sweets or *wheely-trade*?', ie some kind of mechanical toy. Such usage explains a sentence in a nineteenth-century dialect tale from Netherton's *Cornish Almanac*: 'The *apern-trade* all pitched to scraim', ie 'the women-folk all began to scream'. The commonest formation is perhaps *cakey-trade*, ie 'confectionery' or 'cakestuffs in general': 'Where 'tis,' I once heard someone explain, 'they don't go in across much cakey-trade up the country', ie 'less cakestuff is eaten in England'. This, incidentally, is a fact. There must be many 'foreigners' who, like the character in one of Q's best short-stories 'Step o' One Side' (an amusing evocation of tensions in a china-clay village), have felt daunted by a look at a 'faith tea' and have found that the first word that came into their mind was 'fattening'.

Doctor's trade is medicine. 'In Rhode Island,' wrote John S. Farmer, the nineteenth-century expert on slang, 'medicine is strangely termed trade.' This does not seem strange in Devon and Cornwall.

TREGEAGLE

There are times when the English teacher is called upon to perform with his class the exercise of completing similes – 'as thin as a rake', 'as fat as a pig' etc. Faced, in the past, with this rather mechanical chore, I have often wished I could enliven the proceedings by importing some of the more vivid dialect comparisons I have heard, now fast dying out: 'as sour as a crab' for instance (ie a crab-apple); 'as drunk as a hand-cart'; 'as deep as Dolcoath mine' (*deep,* usually, as applied to people in the somewhat sinister sense of 'subtle, reserved, having hidden depths'); 'as dark as a dog's guts', or 'as dark as a bag' (Devonian rather than Cornish, and accordingly pronounced *beg*); 'as tough as ling' (the fish, that is, not the plant); 'as full as a egg' (generally used of clouds which are threatening, or *banking up* to bring rain); 'as teasy's a snake'; 'as quick as a cooper round a cask' (this from North Devon, with interesting insight into a dying craft) and finally, the common 'as daft (or ironically 'as smart') as a carrot half scraped'.

Perhaps the most interesting Cornish simile of all is that whereby a loud noise, the sound of the wind, for example, or of a child crying, is said to be 'like Tregeagle'. 'Roaring like Tregeagle' is still a usual phrase. Tregeagle, who flourished in the Cromwellian period, was an unjust and cruel bailiff of the lords of Lanhydrock, and he has had grafted on to him several legends perhaps formerly attributed to the devil. In atonement for his sins while alive, he must still drain Dozmary Pool, in the bleakest part of Bodmin Moor, with a leaky limpet-shell. Driven by devils, he can be heard howling on windy nights, with his head through the 'big window' of

Roche Rock. The family and house which he founded at Trevorder did not prosper, but memorials to his son and grandson, though not to Tregeagle himself, are to be found in the church at St Breock, in the 'lewth' of the St Breock downs (or *St Bregg* downs, as they are pronounced locally).

UGLY

Reversing the usual process of definition, we may say that standard English *ugly* means, in dialect phrase, 'behind the door when good looks was gived out'. I do not know that this condition is especially common in the South West, but we have some nicely graded comparisons for it. An *ugly jug* is 'a Toby jug', and 'a good face for an ugly jug' will serve for a normal amount of plainness. For a severer case, 'a face like a diseased boot' may answer; while in an extreme instance we could call upon, 'a face like a chield's arse after nine days' slapping'.

But perhaps one would only resort to the last phrase if one were feeling *ugly* in the special dialect sense of 'bad-tempered, in an ugly or vindictive mood'. In this sense people in a family feud, for instance, are said to 'turn ugly' – not remaining on speaking terms, perhaps. *Ghastly* can have a similar meaning, though it is not recorded in the *EDD*. Whole families can have a reputation for this and other vices, leaving neighbours to come up with the excuse – or at least the explanation – which can only be offered in the kind of close community that villages are rapidly ceasing to be, that the trait is a family failing: 'Of course, you must remember, he's a W—, D—, P—, T— . . .'

Not all people, however, are remarkable for their vices, or their vindictiveness. A man can be *comfortable,* that is, 'easy to get along with', or a *proper* chap. Perhaps the ultimate sign of acceptability, however, and a very desirable distinction for the middle-aged and elderly, is to be referred to generally in the community as 'Uncle' or 'Aunt', even by those to whom one is not related. I should guess that Uncle Tom Cobley from the song 'Widecombe Fair' had this status. This now fast-dying tradition may go back to medieval times, and it occurs also in the Cornish language – if that eccentric Victorian poet and Anglo-Catholic clergyman, Hawker of Morwenstow, is to be believed: 'They were wont, on the Tamar side, to call the Mother of God, in their loyal language, Modryb Maria, or Aunt Mary.' I have yet to meet an example of *Modryb* (or *Modryp*) *Maria* in a Cornish text and we badly need a proper Cornish dictionary furnished with references to the surviving works; but what does lend some credence to Hawker's statement are some traditional words to the tune of the Helston Furry Dance, collected in the last century:

> God bless Aunt Mary Moses
> And all her power and might O!
> And send us peace in merry England
> Send peace by day and night, O!

Aunt Mary Moses may well be a corruption of *Modryb Maria*.

UPON

Upon is common in dialect, often where standard English makes do with *on*. 'To have pissed 'pon a nettle' means 'to be bad-tempered'. The devil is said to 'piss 'pon the brembles' after Michaelmas Day, which accounts for the rapid deterioration in the quality of blackberries from that date. 'What are you on upon' is a redundant and suspicious phrase, meaning 'What sort of game are you playing?' 'Come 'pon that' is still a common alternative for 'if it comes to that' – three words instead of five.

Another expression much used for its brevity is *better fit*, meaning 'it would be more suitable if'. Anne Treneer quotes a Bible Christian who reprimanded her father, the schoolmaster at Gorran, for reading fairy stories with the children: 'Better fit the children read their Bibles than old lies!'

VAMP

In the last war the country was urged to 'make do and mend'. It was something that came naturally to Cornishmen, who were often amazed at the extravagance of Londoners and evacuees. Mr Harry Gregory, the noted *wrassler,* told me how flabbergasted he was at the luxurious living he encountered when, between the wars, he visited London in order to give a display of *wrasslin,* under the auspices of promoter Jack Solomons, and was put up at a West End hotel. 'Sixpence, they charged to clean your shoes, if you please! I said, "Sixpence would buy mother a tin of Cherry Blossom, keep our shoes clean for 'ears." '

A word that bears out this habit of mind is the word *vamp.* It meant to knit new parts on to a *stocking* (the word includes 'sock'), perhaps even a new foot to an existing leg. Such were the habits of what were formerly known as *steracoose* women, ie 'energetic and contriving'. Hence the noun *vamp* comes to mean the whole article, 'a sock'. In a very authentic-sounding short-story of West Cornwall called 'How Martha didn't marry a Sumpman', when Martha's fiancé is injured in a tin-mine accident she says philosophically, 'Awnly a leg gone. And what's that? Awnly a boot less to clane and shine up, and a vamp less to knit and mend.'

If the word occurs in the dialect at all now (apart from its standard English use of extemporising an accompaniment on a piano) it is used with the allied sense of adding extra drink, from a tea-pot or bottle, to strengthen a half-empty cup or glass. Professor Ross and Miss Nancy Mitford tell us that the non-U equivalent of 'Have some more tea?' is 'How is your cup?' A still more non-U dialectal variant in the South West might be, 'Shall I vamp your cup?' Some Victorian glossaries record a verb to *Cornish together,* for when all the company drinks out of the same cup or glass, but this I have never heard. There are limits to unrefinement, even in mid-Cornwall.

A special challenge to the economical was provided by the killing of a pig. People boasted that they used up everything of the pig 'except the squeal'. Miss Courtney notes the custom of throwing the pig's nose over the house for luck: 'This is how it was done. The lady took the nose of a pig, that was killed the day before, in her right hand, stood with her back to the house, and threw the nose over her head, and over the house, into the back garden. Had she failed in the attempt her luck was supposed to be bad.' Incidentally, Miss Courtney records this custom from Summercourt, which she describes as 'East Cornwall'. Many people born West of Truro divide the County in this way. I know one Penzance woman who refers to the hundreds of Penwith and Kerrier as 'The West of England'. Professor Charles Thomas quotes the Camborne saying of older Dolcoath men: 'Beyond Truro, where they d'have the treacle mines', ie 'nowhere'.

'VUZZ'

'He got a little place out of coor (ie he has a smallholding which he works when he is not on a shift).' Nothing is more characteristic of older Cornwall and West Devon than this arrangement; a few acres of ground as a second string to one's bow in case the clay-work or the mine 'went scat'. Many of the liveliest comparisons in the dialect reflect such a background; a moorland smallholding with a small rick or *pook* of turf (peat) for fuel and perhaps another of *vuzz* (ie 'furze' – *gorse* tends to be a more northern word) for the heating of the cloam oven. One could still see such a pair of ricks until recently on the Bodmin moors. Hence dialect expressions like 'a great pook of turf' for a fat woman, or 'like a vuzz-rick' to describe dishevelled hair. People's clothes, if creased and crumpled, are said to be 'like if the calves been sucking of 'em'. Devon has a comparable phrase recorded by Mrs Hewett: 'You've a-cramed your vroks purty well . . . They luke's though they'd been drawed dru a calve's mouth.' The prudent put on their oldest clothes to feed 'scald' milk to the calves, who have a habit of butting (in dialect *bunching*) the feeder in a friendly but messy way.

The associations of furze are with barren, unproductive countryside. An old rhyme, which may have heartened Saltash in combating the 'big-brother' tactics of Plymouth, runs:

> Saltash was a borough town
> When Plymouth was a vuzzy down.

The same observation has been made of 'Kirton' (Crediton) and Exeter. Nevertheless, there was money in furze. Mrs

M. Cuddy, recorder of St Just and Pendeen Old Cornwall Society, provided me with an interesting old table for the measurement of furze, an important source of fuel in former times. Two *tasks* (handfuls) laid together with the prickles at opposite ends and tied in the middle made one *faggot*; seven faggots made one *truss*. Two trusses, one each side, were as much as a pony or donkey could carry. She quotes a farmer's day-book for the 1830s which records £40 being made in one year by selling furze in this way.

Reverting, however, to the word with which we began, *place*, besides meaning a smallholding, can also be used in a grandiose way for a central area surrounded by cottages in even the smallest hamlets. Trezaise Town Place, for instance, was such a microcosm. It even has, or had until recently, a 'big house' to which the owners of smaller cottages nearby looked with respect and for occasional charity; yet there were fewer than a dozen houses all told.

Different again, and probably influenced by, if not derived from, Celtic Cornish *plas*, 'a palace', is the usage of *place* to refer to the Squire's house in towns like Padstow and Fowey – in this instance Prideaux Place and Place House respectively. They doubtless would have seemed like palaces in former times, compared to the hovels that then surrounded them.

WANT

Occasionally one meets a word that is so widespread in dialects as to be barely dialectal at all. Such a word is *want*, a variant for 'mole', found in most Midlands and southern counties. The word is mentioned by one of the earliest Cornishmen whose English writings have come down to us – John of Trevisa, translator, in 1387, of a *Polychronicon* (a sort of encyclopedic history) by Ranulph Higden. One sentence to the effect that there are no moles in Ireland runs, 'There lacketh wontes and othere venemous bestes.'

As the *SED* shows, the pronunciation with a rounded vowel, suggested by Trevisa's spelling here, is closer to that found in the western rather than in the middle or eastern parts of

Cornwall. Elsewhere than in the far west the word rhymes with *pant*. The point is nicely illustrated in Miss Courtney's *Cornish Feasts and Folk-Lore*: 'Once in the Land's End district I overtook an old man and asked him what had made so many hillocks in a field through which we were passing. His answer was, "What you rich people never have in your houses – wants." ' This bitter pun would hardly have been possible, for phonetic reasons, in Mid or East Cornwall.

WEAR'TH THE TROUSERS

Probably the most striking evidence of the decline of dialect in the West that the recent *SED* reveals is the almost total eclipse of the old historical ending of the third person singular *-th* (as in *saith, doth* etc), still familiar to us in archaic usage from the Bible, but almost vanished from dialect. That comparative newcomer, the ending in *-s, (says, does)* is almost universal. It seems from the *SED* that North-East Cornwall (round about Kilkhampton) is almost the only place in the whole of England where it was surviving in the 1950s. There, a domineering woman was characterised to the fieldworkers with the words, 'Her wear'th the trousers.'

What a different state of affairs from late Victorian and Edwardian times! In an article of 1891 on the dialect of Hartland, the following doggerel was quoted to illustrate the 'almost invariable' third person ending:

> Yur liv'th Bill Cruse,
> A mak'th gude shoes,
> A tak'th the best of leather.
> A zaw'th mun strong,
> (they must last long)
> So a put'th mun well together.

The point was also a distinguishing mark of East, as opposed to West Cornwall dialect. In that (for its author) rather sensational novel *The Birthright,* by Joseph Hocking, the hero is kidnapped, blindfolded and imprisoned he knows not where. But when his female jailer admonishes him with 'Ait yer mait' and then later says, 'Who is there that knaweth?', he deduces from her pronunciation that he is in Cornwall and from her grammar that he is in the eastern half.

More detailed evidence on this point, in fact a rather valuable, though neglected, piece of evidence for Cornish dialects in their heyday, is provided by the Reverend Mark Guy Pearse in the Victorian best-seller *Daniel Quorm and His Religious Notions* (*2nd series*), part of which turns on the conflict between Daniel, a West Cornwall Methodist, and Farmer Gribble, as East Cornwall Anglican. Such differentiating features as the voicing of 'f' and 's' as 'v' and 'z', the unrounding of 'o' to 'a', the characteristic pronunciation, east of Pydar and Powder hundreds, of words like *two* and *you* with a Devon-type vowel (suggested by spellings like *tew*), as well as this old inflexion -*th* for the eastern half of the county, are richly illustrated. Moreover they are contrasted with West Cornwall speech which, as Pearse realised, was much nearer to standard English because English was acquired in the far west comparatively late:

A 'I 'moast a-vorgot what I comed for. Tez the strap; et wan'th a stitch or tew, zo Bill zaith.'

B 'That's soon done,' said Daniel . . . 'There, Mest' Gribble; if broken hearts were mended so easy as that, 'twould be a different world from what 'tis.'

Speaker A here is East Cornwall, speaker B is West Cornwall; though in his proselytising zeal (Farmer Gribble, of course, turns Methodist) I suspect the reverend author of making Daniel Quorm speak less in dialect than a West Cornwall shoemaker of the time normally would.

'WESSLEAN'

In those parts of England where the British population has always been considerable, some accentuation from the ancient language has persisted. But dialect speakers, I fear, who retain in their pronunciation of proper names a stress which makes sense in the original Celtic languages, are fighting a losing battle against 'the media'. The stress on purely English compound names is, of course, on the first element. It would be foolish to pronounce Blackpool as Black*pool,* since what distinguished the original pool was doubtless its blackness. But it would be equally foolish to stress the *Pol* in Poldhu, our Cornish 'Blackpool', made famous in 1901 when Marconi received wireless signals from there in Newfoundland.

The BBC announcer now manages to shelve the problem in all difficult instances, and some which are not really difficult at all, by opting for level stress. A generation ago Holyhead and Penzance – which mean the same thing, the one name in English, the other in Cornish – were accentuated on the first and second element respectively. This was logical, since the distinguishing adjective, here *holy* and *sans,* tends to come before the noun in Germanic languages and after it in Celtic languages. This is the crux of the matter, the reason why so many Celtic words should be pronounced with the accent on the last syllable. Today both Penzance and Holyhead are increasingly likely to be pronounced with level stress, even by a member of a distinguished old Cornish family like TV newsreader Kenneth Kendall.

But there is a worse habit – that of pronouncing Cornish names with an entirely English accentuation. For example, the name Redruth is often enunciated as if one were talking of a scarlet woman, or the Cornish Lis*keard* given the same accentuation as the Cheshire *Lis*card. Strictly the Celticist may object in this instance that these last two names are both Celtic, having as their first element Cornish *lis* and Welsh *llys* respectively, both meaning 'court, hall'. But Cheshire has been thoroughly Anglicised, whereas the Celtic accent in Cornwall has been strong enough in the past to tip the balance even with two English name-elements, as in Wade*bridge,* still locally accented the opposite way from *Wey*bridge in Surrey.

The most remarkable instance of the tenacity of this Celtic accentuation is the pronunciation of the English adjective Wesleyan, which the Cornish have made peculiarly their own by accenting not the first syllable of Wesley but the second – 'Wess*léan*'.

One very frequent apparent exception to this rule about the accentuation of the last syllable is *hendra,* meaning 'old house' or 'old place'; but in fact this in some way proves the rule, as for once, in both Welsh and Cornish the adjective (*hen*) precedes the noun.

The first great authority on the Cornish language, Henry Jenner, writing at the beginning of this century, noted this tendency to Anglicise Cornish names: 'There is a Mr Roseveare of my acquaintance who is of the second generation away from Cornwall, and is always called *Rose*vear, not Rose*vear*. Yet in Cornwall no one ever misplaces the accent, even on a name that he has never heard before. There seems to be an instinctive understanding, a sort of ghost of the old language still hovering around its old habitation.'

WHAT HO!

For over 100 years now education has been compulsory for all. No doubt, up to a point, this has made us more literate; it has certainly made spoken English more uniform. But it often happens that the words, phrases and forms which the primary school teacher banishes from the classroom, and even – if he can – from the playground, have quite a respectable ancestry. I well remember being told at school that certain expressions were only heard from people who aspired no higher than to be farm-labourers all their lives. One of the under-teachers was very emphatic that we should eschew the westcountry greetings 'What ho!' and 'What cheer!' – so common in Shakespeare.

I do not know what he would have made of the vulgar greetings, still occasionally heard, 'Can 'ee sweat?' A. K. Hamilton-Jenkin makes quite a lot of this phrase:

> This curious greeting, formerly used among the 'bal maidens' (mine girls) may possibly be reminiscent of the days when cholera was rife and when to ask a person if he could sweat was synonymous to inquiring if he were in good health.

WIDDLES

Reading dialect glossaries and dictionaries soon demonstrates how very far the old rural society was from being 'permissive'.

The consensus was all for morality, propriety, prosperity and general effectiveness, and many words were minted with the express purpose of giving short shrift to lame ducks. All told, quite a proportion of the *EDD* must be taken up with terms for penalties and punishments, many of them corporal. 'I'll *scat* at 'ee, *lam* to 'ee, *wuzz* at 'ee, give 'ee a *duff in th'ear*, a good *leathering, larruping, lacing*' – these are common in the South West, though not all confined to that area. A favourite threat of one old carpenter was 'I'll measure your arse with my rule!'

Even superstitions and omens could have an underlying moral and practical purpose. To tell a girl who got her apron wet when she first helped with washing clothes that she would marry a drunkard might not be reliable forecasting, but it probably encouraged her to take more care; as also the advice to the feckless who did not mend their clothes until they came to put them on:

> Mend a rag on your back
> You'll never be a penny better than your pack.

The womenfolk retained many such saws and superstitions, which were often contemptuously dismissed by menfolk as 'old women's widdles'.

This last word is interesting. In the last of the three plays of the Cornish *Ordinalia,* the play of the Resurrection, Mary Magdalene's assertion that she has seen her risen Lord is silenced by the doubter, Thomas, with the words 'tav ty wrek gans the *whethlow*' – 'Silence, thou woman, with thy *widdles*' (Welsh *chwedl*).

WISHT

Here, at least, is a word which still thrives and may even be gaining ground. It occurs as an adjective meaning 'dismal, melancholy, ill, sad, poor', and is common also as an intensive to *poor*: 'a *wisht poor* yield of taties'. Bishop Latimer (c1490–1555), who would have gone down well, with his racy sermons, on any Cornish 'plan', used the word to describe the way the guests of Adonaijah, heir-apparent to David, all forsook him when the dying David preferred his younger son Solomon: 'And when they perceived that Solomon, by the advice of

his father, was anointed king, by and by there was all whisht.'
Two-and-a-half centuries later, on 5 August 1796, Elizabeth
Clift of Bodmin describes in a letter her new 'situation' with
the Reverend Mr Coffin of Linkinghorne: 'It is the wishtes
(sic) place you ever saw.' And today, when, as so often happens
in the West, Monday mornings are moist and muggy, the
housewife says ' 'Tis wisht dryth today.' 'The relative humidity
is unfavourable to the drying of laundry' – that is what *wisht
dryth* means; so it may well survive, having brevity to
commend it. (*Dryth* is used, by the way, only of climate; no
one would say, 'Feel the dryth of these clothes.')

But the word *wisht,* like a few other dialect expressions,
still retains deeper overtones:

'How is she then?'
'She's wisht; goin' home fast!'

In such contexts dialect is not, as it so often appears, the vehicle
of rustic comedy. We tend to forget that until recently, and
perhaps still in remote places and on intimate occasions, dialect
words are not merely marginal comments in apologetic inverted
commas, or the retailed oddities of village characters. In the
British Museum there is a copy, one of a limited edition of 250,
of *The Song of Solomon* as rendered in a rather generalised
Cornish dialect of 1859. Here is one of the more memorable
passages (8 : 7) as given in the King James Bible of 1611.

Many waters cannot quench love; neither can the floods
drown it; if a man would give all the substance of his house
for love, it would be utterly condemned.

And in the dialect version:

Many waters caan't quinch love, ne'ther can the floods drown
et; ef a man would give all the traade in his house for love,
'wouldn't be no use 'tall.

The translator is hampered by the already-overworked and
illogical spelling of standard English, but we are still aware,
as we read this, of the depth of feeling which a despised and
vanishing vernacular can still convey.

If all these dialect expressions were forgotten, ' 'twould be
a wisht poor job, sure 'nough'.

REFERENCES AND NOTES

The following notes refer chiefly to quoted material, though in a few instances they document salient statements of fact. In the case of quotations, the catchwords used below are always the last words of the passage quoted. In the case of statements of fact, a word central to the idea is used as one of the catchwords.

The following abbreviations are used:

EDD	*The English Dialect Dictionary*
EETS, es	Early English Text Society, extra series
EETS, os	Early English Text Society, original series
ME	Middle English (c1150 to 1470)
OC	*Old Cornwall* (magazine of the Federation of Old Cornwall Societies)
OE	Old English (up to 1150)
OED	*The Oxford English Dictionary*
SED	*Survey of English Dialects (Southern Counties)*

INTRODUCTION

our rustic dress and manners: Munby, *Man of Two Worlds*, ed Derek Hudson (London, 1972), p67

with her ear-rings: Hilda Rowse, 'Once You start Meddling with Charms', *Cornish Nation* (March 1972)

there edn' no moon: Charles Lee, *Our Little Town* (London, 1909), p15

expect to find them: Sir John Betjeman, *First and Last Loves* (London, 1952), p214

facts and philosophies: Silas K. Hocking, *One in Charity* (London, 1893), chap 2

in severe weather: Gilbert White, *The Natural History of Selborne*, ed Grant Allen (London, 1900), p198

scilicet by jirkes: John Aubrey, *Brief Lives*, ed Andrew Clark (Oxford, 1898), II.25

thare owle erdingstowe: The Owl and the Nightingale (EETS, es 119), 1.25

I do not know: Bernard Walke, *Twenty Years at St. Hilary*
(London, 1935), p19
Appropriateness of the comparison: This word, *fert,* both literally
and figuratively a four-letter word, has never, so far as I know,
been recorded. *Fert-worms* are tape-worms: 'You'm wriggling
like anybody with the fert-worms!' It is possible, though not
polite, to conclude a bantering argument with this monosyllable
'Old Mr Trebilcock': Anne Treneer, *Happy Button* (London,
1950)
Mr W. J. Hawken: Will J. Hawken, *Shiner's Poems* (Oxford, 1974)

ABROAD

carring . . . the hay: The loss of *y* or *i* when it is the first of two
vowels is characteristic. *Spaniel* is often pronounced as *span'l;*
or we can compare the chorus of the song 'Widecombe Fair',
in which *Dan'l* Whiddon appears

BACKALONG

whenever I've a mind to: OC (VI, 104)
in Okehampton: M. B. Harris, 'Relationships of Place in a Devonshire Dialect', *Archivum Linguisticum,* ns (1970), p43–8
extremity of Newlyn: OC (11, 8.22)

BELONG

belonged to Mr Prout: F. Rilstone, 'The Dialect Use of the Verb
"Belong"', *Devon and Cornwall Notes and Queries,* XXIII
(1948), p169–70

BRIEF

a brief 'n tes to work: F. T. Elworthy, *The Dialect of West
Somerset* (London, 1875–86), I. 91

BRYANITES

William O. Bryan: 'The name is spelt "Bryan", "Brian", "Bryant"
according to preference, and young William was to add a
further variation when he adopted the form "O'Bryan" on
account of a supposed Irish ancestry which the known facts do
not support.' Thomas Shaw, *The Bible Christians* (London,
1965), p3
the place for the chapel: F. W. Bourne, *Billy Bray, The King's
Son* (London, 1937), p51

CAP'N

fifteenth century: See The Wesleys in Cornwall: Extracts from

the Journals of John and Charles Wesley, ed John Pearce
(Truro, 1964), p52n

from Shropshire to Cornwall: cf *The Winter's Tale,* III.iii

CLICKY

right-handed or clicky: EDD, s.v. *click* (adj). In the fourth century
AD, Ulfilas, translating the Greek version of St Matthew's gospel
into the earliest recorded Germanic language of Gothic, renders
'left hand' in Matthew 6: 3 ('Let not thy left hand know what
thy right hand doeth') as *hleidumei.* Since, by Grimm's law,
Gothic *h* corresponds to *c* in the non-Germanic languages,
Gothic *hleidumei* and Cornish *cledhek* are seen to be related,
and our dialect word *clicky,* it appears, is of Indo-European
age.

on her clean clothes: Kate Roberts, 'Chwiorydd', *Rhigolau Bywyd*
(Aberystwyth, 1929), p49

CLUNK

llwnc o de: Kate Roberts, 'Pryfocio', *O Gors y Bryniau* (Wrexham,
1926), p89

DOWNSER

moor often had this meaning: OC (VI, 394)
jarring voices bent: Spenser, *Virgil's Gnat,* 1.230

FIGGY HOBBAN

middle of it and baked: Faria Risom, 'How Martha didn't Marry
a Sumpman', *Longman's Magazine,* XXI (1893), p375–91

HER AND US

the old hundred boundaries: M. Wakelin, *Patterns in the Folk-
Speech of the British Isles* (London, 1972), p3

KNUCKLY-DOWNS

knuckly down 'pon one knee: A. L. Rowse, *A Cornishman at
Oxford* (London, 1965), p91
it was sloany-pie: Sloan, a dialect form of *sloe* still occasionally
heard, is from the Old English plural *slan,* misunderstood as a
singular.
*has been anointed: Bewnans Meriasek: The Life of St. Meriasek,
Bishop and Confessor. A Cornish Drama,* ed Whitley Stokes
(London, 1872), 1. 3412

for thirty sterling: Ordinalia: Passio, 1. 1552
His face and His two eyes: ibid, 1. 1393

LEWTH

Rosemanoweth was in the lewth: Ann Treneer, *Happy Button* (London, 1950), p62. The change in attitude to the siting of houses was doubtless partly brought about by the writings of William Gilpin on the Picturesque. It begins to be noticeable in the early nineteenth century, if not before. Here is Mr Parker, a character in Jane Austen's unfinished novel, *Sanditon:* 'Our ancestors, you know, always built in a hole. Here were we, pent down in this little contracted nook, without air or veiw (sic), only one mile from the noblest expanse of ocean between the South Foreland and the Land's End, and without the smallest advantage from it.' Jane Austen, *Minor Works* (ed Chapman), p380

Man's Days: Published in *The Cornish Magazine* (1898), ed Quiller-Couch, Vol 1, p41, and reprinted in *The Oxford Book of Twentieth-Century Verse*, chosen by Philip Larkin (Oxford, 1973), p53

LOGGAN

from logging to loggan: W. B. Lockwood, 'On Celtic Loan-Words in Modern English', *Zeitschrift fur Anglistick und Amerikanistik*, XIII (1965), p261–75

LOUSTER

Man and woman likewise: Ordinalia: Passio, 1. 2807

LUE!

in Suffolk: A. O. D. Claxton, *The Suffolk Dialect of the Twentieth Century* (Ipswich, 1968), s.v. *loo*

MAIDENS

in the marriage market: OC (V, 16)

MAZED

this is no mazed man: John Wesley, *Journal*, ed N. Curnock (London, 1909), IV. 132
clamour which may be heard a mile: White, op cit, p69

MAZZARD

the beast remained impounded: H. M. Creswell Payne, 'Cornish Pounds', *OC* (IV, 143–7) *that Jane Austen sometimes used:* K. C. Phillipps, *Jane Austen's English* (London, 1970), p153

"OBBY 'OSS'

in No-man's land: Sir John Betjeman, *First and Last Loves,* 223–4

Feast of Lupercal: See Thurstan Peter, 'The Hobby Horse', *Journal of the Royal Institution of Cornwall,* XIX (1915), p241–73

PADGY-POW

nestle-dris and nestle-tripe: Interesting maps for the nation-wide variation in words for 'newt' and for 'the weakest pig of the litter' will be found in G. L. Brook, *English Dialects* (London, 1963)

found throughout the county: Wakelin, *English Dialects: An Introduction* (London, 1972), p128–9

a fine girl of her: I am indebted for these Welsh parallels to Mr Brinley Rees of Bangor

PUT AND TAKE

With a procession put thee: Bewnans Meriasek, 1. 1858

QUAILAWAY

needes must quaile: Spenser, *The Shepherd's Calendar,* November, 1. 91

RATTLE-CUM-SKIT

Celtic Cornish: See M. Wakelin, *'Crew, cree* and *crow:* Celtic Words in an English Dialect', *Anglia,* LXXXVII (1969), p273-81

SCRUFF

on the cold canvas: Linoleum is a trade name, appearing first in the 1870s, for canvas specially treated with oxidised linseed oil. Earlier, our dialectal *canvas* had been the word; 'I laid *canvas* on the passage, and carpets on the stairs': Charlotte Brontë, *Jane Eyre,* chap 34

SLIGHT

face is her best limb: Courtney, *A Glossary of Words in Use in Cornwall* (London, 1880), s.v. *slight*

the evil angel: Bewnans Meriasek, 1. 969

with smeech and smoke: Mark Guy Pearse, *Daniel Quorm and his Religious Notions* (London, 1876), chap 6

STUG

the Romane Flood: Spenser, *The Faerie Queene*, VII. vii. 42

Never prosper, boy nor man: M. Courtney, *Cornish Feasts and Folk-lore* (Penzance, 1890), p163

'VUZZ'

in dialect 'bunching': We can compare the action of a rascally Pardoner in *Piers Plowman* (A text), 1. 71:

'Lewide men leuide hym wel and likide his speche;
Comen vp knelynge to kissen his bulle.
He *bunchide* hem with his breuet and blered here eiyen.'

WEAR'TH THE TROUSERS

put'th mun well together: R. Pears Chope, 'The Dialect of Hartland', *Transactions of the Devon Association*, XXIII (1891), p420–9

different world from what 'tis: Pearse, *Daniel Quorm and his Religious Notions*, second series (London, 1885), chap 8

'WESSLEAN'

around its old habitation: Henry Jenner, 'Some Rough Notes on the Pronunciation of Cornish Names', *Revue Celtique*, XXIV (1903), p300–5

WIDDLES

with thy widdles: Ordinalia: Resurrectio, 1. 901

ACKNOWLEDGEMENTS

My first and best thanks must go to my wife Patricia who has helped with the production of this book at all stages. To call her a research assistant would be a gross understatement! It would have been a pleasure, also, but it is now a sad duty, to pay tribute to the late Professor Melville Richards, formerly Head of the Department of Welsh Language and Literature at the University College of North Wales, Bangor, where I spent a term of study-leave, profiting from the sound teaching of his Department, and the excellent library attached to it. I am particularly grateful to Mr Brinley Rees, of Bangor, who was most generous with his time in assisting me in my struggles with modern Welsh and Middle Cornish. I am also indebted to the library staffs of Leicester University, the British Museum, the Bodleian, the Royal Institution of Cornwall, Truro, and the Methodist Archives and Research Centre in the City Road.

Much of the material in this book has appeared already in that most civilised of daily papers, *The Western Morning News*, and I am grateful to the editor for permission to reprint it; as also, for the same reason, to the editors of the *Journal of the Royal Institution of Cornwall*, and of *Cornish Studies*, the periodical published by the recently formed Institute of Cornish Studies. I have been both encouraged and informed by a large number of letters from readers in Devon and Cornwall and also in New Zealand, where some of my articles have been reprinted by 'cousin Jacks', as Cornish exiles are called. Mrs Kathleen Hawke of Trethurgy, St Austell, but formerly from West Cornwall, and the Reverend T. W. M. Darlington from the Okehampton area, lent me their dialect glossaries, both of which merit publication. Dr Frances Austen, of Liverpool, gave permission to reproduce some quotations from the Clift family papers (Bodmin), which she is in process of editing. Finally, I should like to thank my colleagues at Leicester, Dr J. R. Watson and Miss Monica Jones, who read the typescript and made many valuable suggestions. Any errors, however, whether of fact or judgement, are entirely my own.

INDEX